THE TRANSPARENCY OF
EVIL

THE TRANSPARENCY OF
EVIL

Essays on Extreme Phenomena

Jean Baudrillard

Translated by James Benedict

London · New York

First published as *La transparence du mal: Essai sur les phénomènes extrèmes*
© Editions Galilée, Paris 1990
This translation first published by Verso 1993
Paperback edition reprinted 1993, 1995, 1996, 1999, 2000, 2002
Translation © James Benedict 1993

Verso
UK: 6 Meard Street, London W1F 0EG
USA: 180 Varick Street, New York, NY 10014-4606

Verso is the imprint of New Left Books

ISBN 0-86091-387-2
ISBN 0-86092-588-3 (pbk)

British Library Cataloguing in Publication Data
A catalogue record for this book is available from the British Library

Library of Congress Cataloging-in-Publication Data
A catalogue record for this book is available from the Library of Congress

Typeset by York House Typographic Ltd
Printed and bound in Great Britain by
The Bath Press, Bath

CONTENTS

PART II: RADICAL OTHERNESS

TRANSLATOR'S ACKNOWLEDGEMENTS

For all kinds of vital help in the preparation of this translation, I must, once again, offer heartfelt thanks to M. N. Many thanks, also, to Malcolm Imrie and Lucy Morton, my editors at Verso.

James Benedict

PART I

Since the world is on a delusional course, we must adopt a delusional standpoint towards the world.

Better to die from extremes than starting from the extremities.

AFTER THE ORGY

If I were asked to characterize the present state of affairs, I would describe it as 'after the orgy'. The orgy in question was the moment when modernity exploded upon us, the moment of liberation in every sphere. Political liberation, sexual liberation, liberation of the forces of production, liberation of the forces of destruction, women's liberation, children's liberation, liberation of unconscious drives, liberation of art. The assumption of all models of representation, as of all models of anti-representation. This was a total orgy – an orgy of the real, the rational, the sexual, of criticism as of anti-criticism, of development as of the crisis of development. We have pursued every avenue in the production and effective overproduction of objects, signs, messages, ideologies and satisfactions. Now everything has been liberated, the chips are down, and we find ourselves faced collectively with the big question: WHAT DO WE DO NOW THE ORGY IS OVER?

Now all we can do is simulate the orgy, simulate liberation. We may pretend to carry on in the same direction, accelerating, but in reality we are accelerating in a void, because all the goals of liberation are already behind us, and because what haunts and obsesses us is being thus ahead of all the results – the very availability of all the signs, all the forms, all the desires that we had been pursuing. But what can we do? This is the state of simulation, a state in which we are obliged to replay all scenarios precisely because they have all taken place already, whether actually or potentially. The state of utopia realized, of all utopias realized, wherein paradoxically we must continue to live as though they had not been. But since they have, and since we can no longer, therefore, nourish the hope of realizing them, we can only 'hyper-realize' them through interminable simulation. We live amid the interminable reproduction of ideals, phantasies, images and dreams which are now behind us, yet which we must continue to reproduce in a sort of inescapable indifference.

The fact is that the revolution has well and truly happened, but not in the way we expected. Everywhere what has been liberated has been liberated so that it can enter a state of pure circulation, so that it can go into orbit. With the benefit of a little hindsight, we may say that the unavoidable goal of all liberation is to foster and provision circulatory networks. The fate of the things liberated is an incessant commutation, and these things are thus subject to increasing indeterminacy, to the principle of uncertainty.

Nothing (not even God) now disappears by coming to an end, by dying. Instead, things disappear through proliferation or contamination, by becoming saturated or transparent, because of extenuation or extermination, or as a result of the epidemic of simulation, as a result of their transfer into the secondary existence of simulation. Rather than a mortal mode of disappearance, then, a fractal mode of dispersal.

Nothing is truly reflected any more – whether in a mirror or in the abyssal realm (which is merely the endless reduplication of consciousness). The logic of viral dispersal in networks is no longer a logic of value; neither, therefore, is it a logic of equivalence. There is no longer any such thing as a revolution of values – merely a circumvention or involution of values. A centripetal compulsion coexists with a decentredness of all systems, an internal metastasis or fevered endogenic virulence which creates a tendency for systems to explode beyond their own limits, to override their own logic – not in the sense of creating sheer redundancy, but in the sense of an increase in power, a fantastic potentialization whereby their own very existence is put at risk.

All of which brings us back to the fate of value. Once, out of some obscure need to classify, I proposed a tripartite account of value: a natural stage (use-value), a commodity stage (exchange-value), and a structural stage (sign-value). Value thus had a natural aspect, a commodity aspect, and a structural aspect. These distinctions are formal ones, of course – reminiscent of the distinctions between the particles physicists are always coming up with. A new particle does not replace those discovered earlier: it simply joins their ranks, takes its place in a hypothetical series. So let me introduce a new particle into the microphysics of simulacra. For after the natural, commodity, and structural stages of value comes the fractal stage. The first of these stages had a natural referent, and value developed on the basis of a natural use of the world. The second was founded on a general equivalence, and value developed by reference to a logic of the commodity. The third is governed by a code, and value develops here by reference to a set of models. At the fourth, the fractal (or viral, or radiant) stage of value, there is no point of reference at all, and value radiates in all directions, occupying all interstices, without reference to anything whatsoever, by virtue of pure contiguity. At the fractal stage there is no longer any equivalence, whether natural or general. Properly speaking there is now no law of value, merely a sort of *epidemic of value*, a sort of general metastasis of value, a haphazard proliferation and dispersal of value. Indeed, we should really no longer speak of 'value' at all, for this kind of propagation or chain reaction makes all valuation impossible. Once again we are put in mind of microphysics: it is as impossible to make estimations between beautiful and ugly, true and false, or good and evil, as it is simultaneously to calculate a particle's speed and position. Good is no longer the opposite of evil, nothing can now be plotted on a graph or analysed in terms of abscissas and ordinates. Just as each particle follows its own trajectory, each value or fragment of value shines for a moment in the heavens of simulation, then disappears into the void along a crooked path that only rarely happens to intersect with other such paths. This is the pattern of the fractal – and hence the current pattern of our culture.

When things, signs or actions are freed from their respective ideas, concepts, essences, values, points of reference, origins and aims, they embark upon an endless process of self-reproduction. Yet things continue to function long after their ideas have disappeared, and they do so in total indifference to their own content. The paradoxical fact is that they function even better under these circumstances.

Thus, for example, the idea of progress has disappeared, yet progress continues. The idea of wealth that production once connoted has disappeared, yet production itself continues more vigorously than ever. Indeed, it picks up speed precisely in proportion to its increasing indifference to its original aims. Of the political sphere one can say that the idea of politics has disappeared but that the game of politics continues in secret indifference to its own stakes. Of television, that it operates in total indifference to its own images (it would not be affected, in other words, even were mankind to disappear). Could it be that all systems, all individuals, harbour a secret urge to be rid of their ideas, of their own essences, so as to be able to proliferate everywhere, to transport them-selves simultaneously to every point of the compass? In any event, the consequences of a dissociation of this kind can only be fatal. A thing which has lost its idea is like the man who has lost his shadow, and it must either fall under the sway of madness or perish.

This is where the order (or rather, disorder) of metastasis begins – the rule of propagation through mere contiguity, of cancerous proliferation (even the genetic code of value having lost any force). On all sides we witness a kind of fading away of sexuality, of sexual beings, in favour of a return to the earlier (?) stage of immortal and asexual beings reproducing, like protozoa, by simple division of the One into two and the transmission of a code. Today's technological beings – machines, clones, replacement body parts – all tend towards this kind of reproduction, and little by little they are imparting the same process to those beings that are supposedly human, and sexed. The aim everywhere – not least at the leading edge of biological research – is to effect a genetic substitution of this kind, to achieve the linear and sequential reproduction, cloning or parthenogenesis of little celibate machines.

When sexual liberation was the order of the day, the watchword was 'Maximize sexuality, minimize reproduction'. The dream of our present clone-loving society is just the opposite: as much reproduction and as little sex as possible. At one time the body was a metaphor for the soul, then it became a metaphor for sex. Today it is no longer a metaphor for anything at all, merely the locus of metastasis, of the machine-like connections between all its processes, of an endless programming devoid of any symbolic organization or overarching purpose: the body is thus given over to the pure promiscuity of its relationship to itself – the same promiscuity that characterizes networks and integrated circuits.

The possibility of metaphor is disappearing in every sphere. This is an aspect of a general tendency towards transsexuality which extends well beyond sex, affecting all disciplines as they lose their specificity and partake of a process of confusion and contagion – a viral loss of determinacy which is the prime event among all the new events that assail us. Economics becomes transeconomics, aesthetics becomes transaesthetics, sex becomes transsexuality – all converge in a transversal and universal process wherein no discourse may have a metaphorical relationship to another, because for there to be metaphor, differential fields and distinct objects must exist. But they cannot exist where contamination is possible between any discipline and any other. Total metonymy, then – viral by definition (or lack of definition). The viral analogy is *not* an importation from biology, for everything is affected simultaneously and under the same terms by the virulence in question, by the chain reaction we have been discussing, by haphazard and senseless proliferation and metastasis. Perhaps our melancholy stems from this, for metaphor still had its beauty; it was aesthetic, playing as it did upon difference, and upon the illusion of difference. Today, metonymy – replacing the whole as well as the components, and occasioning a general commutability of terms – has built its house upon the dis-illusion of metaphor.

Thus every individual category is subject to contamination, substitution is possible between any sphere and any other: there is a total confusion of types. Sex is no longer located in sex itself, but elsewhere – everywhere else, in fact. Politics is no longer restricted to the political sphere, but infects every sphere – economics, science, art, sport . . . Sport itself, meanwhile, is no longer located in sport as such, but instead in business, in sex, in politics, in the general style of *performance*. All these domains are affected by sport's criteria of 'excellence', effort and record-breaking, as by its childish notion of self-transcendence. Each category thus passes through a phase transition during which its essence is diluted in homeopathic doses, infinitesimal relative to the total solution, until it finally disappears, leaving a trace so small as to be indiscernible, like the 'memory of water'.

AIDS is the reflection not so much of an excess of sex or sexual pleasure as of sex's decompensation through its general spread into all areas of life, its venting through all the trivial variants of sexual incantation. The real loss of immunity concerns sex as a whole, with the disappearance of sexual difference and hence of sexuality *per se*. It is in this diffraction of the sexual reality principle, at the fractal, micrological and non-human level, that the essential confusion of the epidemic takes hold.

Perhaps we still have a memory of sex, rather as water 'remembers' molecules no matter how diluted. But that is the whole point: this is *only* a molecular memory, the corpuscular memory of an earlier life, and not a memory of forms or singularities (water, after all, can hardly retain the features of a face, or the colour of someone's eyes). So what we are left with is the simple imprint of a faceless sexuality infinitely watered down in a broth of politics, media and communications, and eventually manifested in the viral explosion of AIDS.

The law that is imposed on us is the law of the confusion of categories. Everything is sexual. Everything is political. Everything is aesthetic. All at once. Everything has acquired a political meaning, especially since 1968; and it is not just everyday life but also madness, language, the media, even desire, that are politicized as they enter the sphere of liberation, the sphere of mass processes. Likewise everything has become sexual, anything can be an object of desire: power, knowledge – everything is interpreted in terms of phantasies, in terms of repression, and sexual stereotypy reigns in every last corner. Likewise, too, everything is now aestheticized: politics is aestheticized in the spectacle, sex in advertising and porn, and all kinds of activity in what is conventionally referred to as culture – a sort of all-pervasive media- and advertising-led semiologization: 'culture degree Xerox'. Each category is generalized to the greatest possible extent, so that it eventually loses all specificity and is reabsorbed by all the other categories. When everything is political, nothing is political any more, the word itself is meaningless. When everything is sexual, nothing is sexual any more, and sex loses its determinants. When everything is aesthetic, nothing is beautiful or ugly any more, and art itself disappears. This paradoxical state of affairs, which is simultaneously the complete actualization of an idea, the perfect realization of the whole tendency of modernity, and the negation of that idea and that tendency, their annihilation by virtue of their very success, by virtue of their extension beyond their own bounds – this state of affairs is epitomized by a single figure: the transpolitical, the transsexual, the transaesthetic.

There is no longer an avant-garde, political, sexual or artistic, embodying a capacity for anticipation; hence the possibility of any radical critique – whether in the name of desire, of revolution, or of the liberation of forms – no longer exists. The days of that revolutionary movement are gone. The glorious march of modernity has not led to the transformation of all values, as we once dreamed it would, but instead to a dispersal and involution of value whose upshot for us is total confusion – the impossibility of apprehending any determining principle, whether of an aesthetic, a sexual or a political kind.

The proletariat has not succeeded in negating itself as such – the century and a half since Marx has made that clear. The proletariat has failed to negate itself *qua* class and thereby abolish class society *per se*. Perhaps this is because the proletariat never was a class, as had been supposed – because only the bourgeoisie was a true class, and therefore the only one capable of negating itself as such. For it has indeed negated itself, along with capital, and so generated a classless society, albeit one which has nothing to do with the classless society that was supposed to arise from a revolution and from a negation of the proletariat as such. As for the proletariat, it has simply disappeared – vanished along with the class struggle itself. There can be no doubt that had capitalism developed in accordance with its own contradictory logic, it would have been defeated by the proletariat. In an ideal sense, Marx's analysis is still irreproachable. But Marx simply did not foresee that it would be possible for capital, in the face of the imminent threat to its existence, to transpoliticize itself, as it were: to launch itself into an orbit beyond the relations of production and political contradictions, to make itself autonomous in a free-floating, ecstatic and haphazard form, and thus to totalize the world in its own image. Capital (if it may still be so called) has barred the way of political economy and the law of value; it is in this sense that it has successfully escaped its own end. Henceforward it can function independently of its own former aims, and absolutely without reference to any aims whatsoever. The inaugural event of this mutation was undoubtedly the Great Crash of 1929; the stock-market crisis of 1987 was merely an aftershock.

Revolutionary theory also enshrined the living utopian hope that the State would wither away, and that the political sphere would negate itself as such, in the apotheosis of a finally transparent social realm. None of this has come to pass. The political sphere has disappeared, sure enough – but so far from doing so by means of a self-transcendence into the strictly social realm, it has carried that realm into oblivion with it. We are now in the transpolitical sphere; in other words, we have reached the zero point of politics, a stage which also implies the reproduction of politics, its endless simulation. For everything that has not successfully transcended itself can only fall prey to revivals without end. So politics will never finish disappearing – nor will it allow anything else to emerge in its place. A kind of hysteresis of the political reigns.

Art has likewise failed to realize the utopian aesthetic of modern times, to transcend itself and become an ideal form of life. (In earlier times, of course, art had no need of self-transcendence, no need to become a totality, for such a totality already existed – in the shape of religion.) Instead of being subsumed in a transcendent ideality, art has been dissolved within a general aestheticization of everyday life, giving way to a pure circulation of images, a transaesthetics of banality. Indeed, art took this route even before capital, for if the decisive political event was the strategic crisis of 1929, whereby capital debouched into the era of mass transpolitics, the crucial moment for art was undoubtedly that of Dada and Duchamp, that moment when art, by renouncing its own aesthetic rules of the game, debouched into the transaesthetic era of the banality of the image.

Nor has the promised sexual utopia materialized. This was to have con-sisted in the self-negation of sex as a separate activity and its self-realization as total life. The partisans of sexual liberation continue to dream this dream of desire as a totality fulfilled within each of us, masculine and feminine at once, this dream of sexuality as an assumption of desire beyond the difference between the sexes. In point of fact sexual liberation has succeeded only in helping sexuality achieve autonomy as an undifferentiated circulation of the signs of sex. Although we are certainly in transition towards a transsexual state of affairs, this has nothing to do with a revolution of life through sex – and everything to do with a confusion and promiscuity that open the door to virtual indifference (in all senses of the word) in the sexual realm.

Similarly, is not the triumph of communication and information the result of the impossibility of a self-transcendence of the social relationship *qua* alienated relationship? Failing any such transcendence, this relationship can only reiterate itself through communication, proliferating in the proliferation of networks and submitting to the lack of differentiation that characterizes these. Communication is more social than the social itself: it is the hyper-relational, sociality overactivated by social techniques. The social, in its essence, is not this. Rather, it was a dream, a myth, a utopia, a conflicted and contradictory form, a violent form – and, certainly, an occasional and exceptional occurrence. Communication, by banalizing the interface, plunges the social into an undifferentiated state. That is why there is no such thing as a communicational utopia. To conceive of a utopian society based on communication is an impossibility, because communication results, precisely, from a society's inability to transcend itself as a function of new aims. The same goes for information: excess knowledge is dispersed arbitrarily in every direction on the surface, but commutation is the only process to which it is subject. At the interfaces, interlocutors are connected up to one another after the fashion of an electric plug in a socket. Communication 'occurs' by means of a sole instantaneous circuit, and for it to be 'good' communication it must take place fast – there is no time for silence. Silence is banished from our screens; it has no place in communication. Media images (and media texts resemble media images in every way) never fall silent: images and messages must follow one upon the other without interruption. But silence is exactly that – a blip in the circuitry, that minor catastrophe, that slip which, on television for instance, becomes highly meaningful – a break laden now with anxiety, now with jubilation, which confirms the fact that all this communication is basically nothing but a rigid script, an uninterrupted fiction designed to free us not only from the void of the television screen but equally from the void of our own mental screen, whose images we wait on with the same fascination. One day the image of a person sitting watching a television screen voided by a technicians' strike will be seen as the perfect epitome of the anthropological reality of the twentieth century.

TRANSAESTHETICS

We see Art proliferating wherever we turn; talk about Art is increasing even more rapidly. But the soul of Art – Art as adventure, Art with its power of illusion, its capacity for negating reality, for setting up an 'other scene' in opposition to reality, where things obey a higher set of rules, a transcendent figure in which beings, like line and colour on a canvas, are apt to lose their meaning, to extend themselves beyond their own *raison d'être*, and, in an urgent process of seduction, to rediscover their ideal form (even though this form may be that of their own destruction) – in this sense, Art is gone. Art has disappeared as a symbolic pact, as something thus clearly distinct from that pure and simple production of aesthetic values, that proliferation of signs *ad infinitum*, that recycling of past and present forms, which we call 'culture'. There are no more fundamental rules, no more criteria of judgement or of pleasure. In the aesthetic realm of today there is no longer any God to recognize his own. Or, to use a different metaphor, there is no gold standard of aesthetic judgement or pleasure. The situation resembles that of a currency which may not be exchanged: it can only float, its only reference itself, impossible to convert into real value or wealth.

Art, too, must circulate at top speed, and is impossible to exchange. 'Works' of art are indeed no longer exchanged, whether for each other or against a referential value. They no longer have that secret collusiveness which is the strength of a culture. We no longer read such works – we merely decode them according to ever more contradictory criteria.

Nothing in this sphere conflicts with anything else. Neo-Geometrism, Neo-Expressionism, New Abstraction, New Representationalism – all coexist with a marvellous facility amid general indifference. It is only because none of these tendencies has any soul of its own that they can all inhabit the same cultural space; only because they arouse nothing but profound indifference in us that we can accept them all simultaneously.

The art world presents a curious aspect. It is as though art and artistic inspiration had entered a kind of stasis – as though everything which had developed magnificently over several centuries had suddenly been immobilized, paralysed by its own image and its own riches. Behind the whole convulsive movement of modern art lies a kind of inertia, something that can no longer transcend itself and has therefore turned in upon itself, merely repeating itself at a faster and faster rate. On the one hand, then, a stasis of the living form of art, and at the same time a proliferative tendency, wild hyperbole, and endless variations on all earlier forms (the life, moving of itself, of that which is dead). All this is logical enough: where there is stasis, there is metastasis. When a living form becomes disordered, when (as in cancer) a genetically determined set of rules ceases to function, the cells begin to proliferate chaotically. Just as some biological disorders indicate a break in the genetic code, so the present disorder in art may be interpreted as a fundamental break in the secret code of aesthetics.

By its liberation of form, line, colour, and aesthetic notions – as by its mixing up of all cultures, all styles – our society has given rise to a general aestheticization: all forms of culture – not excluding anti-cultural ones – are promoted and all models of representation and anti-representation are taken on board. Whereas art was once essentially a utopia – that is to say, ultimately unrealizable – today this utopia has been realized: thanks to the media, computer science and video technology, everyone is now potentially a creator. Even anti-art, the most radical of artistic utopias, was realized once Duchamp had mounted his bottle-dryer and Andy Warhol had wished he was a machine. All the industrial machinery in the world has acquired an aesthetic dimension; all the world's insignificance has been transfigured by the aestheticizing process.

It is often said that the West's great undertaking is the commercialization of the whole world, the hitching of the fate of everything to the fate of the commodity. That great undertaking will turn out rather to have been the aestheticization of the whole world – its cosmopolitan spectacularization, its transformation into images, its semiological organization. What we are witnessing, beyond the materialist rule of the commodity, is a semio-urgy of everything by means of advertising, the media, or images. No matter how marginal, or banal, or even obscene it may be, everything is subject to aestheticization, culturalization, museumification. Everything is said, everything is exposed, everything acquires the force, or the manner, of a sign. The system runs less on the surplus-value of the commodity than on the aesthetic surplus-value of the sign.

There is much talk of a dematerialization of art, as evidenced, supposedly, by minimalism, conceptual art, ephemeral art, anti-art and a whole aesthetic of transparency, disappearance and disembodiment. In reality, however, what has occurred is a *materialization* of aesthetics everywhere under an operational form. It is indeed because of this that art has been obliged to minimalize itself, to mime its own disappearance. It has been doing this for a century already, duly obeying all the rules. Like all disappearing forms, art seeks to duplicate itself by means of simulation, but it will nevertheless soon be gone, leaving behind an immense museum of artificial art and abandoning the field completely to advertising.

A dizzying eclecticism of form, a dizzying eclecticism of pleasure – such, already, was the agenda of the baroque. For the baroque, however, the vortex of artifice has a fleshly aspect. Like the practitioners of the baroque, we too are irrepressible creators of images, but secretly we are iconoclasts – not in the sense that we destroy images, but in the sense that we manufacture a profusion of images *in which there is nothing to see*. Most present-day images – be they video images, paintings, products of the plastic arts, or audiovisual or synthesized images – are literally images in which there is nothing to see. They leave no trace, cast no shadow, and have no consequences. The only feeling one gets from such images is that behind each one there is something that has disappeared. The fascination of a monochromatic picture is the marvellous absence of form – the erasure, though still in the form of art, of all aesthetic syntax. Similarly, the fascination of transsexuality is the erasure – though in the form of spectacle – of sexual difference. These are images that conceal nothing, that reveal nothing – that have a kind of negative intensity. The only benefit of a Campbell's soup can by Andy Warhol (and it is an immense benefit) is that it releases us from the need to decide between beautiful and ugly, between real and unreal, between transcendence and immanence. Just as Byzantine icons made it possible to stop asking whether God existed – without, for all that, ceasing to believe in him.

This is indeed the miraculous thing. Our images are like icons: they allow us to go on believing in art while eluding the question of its existence. So perhaps we ought to treat all present-day art as a set of rituals, and for ritual use only; perhaps we ought to consider art solely from an anthropological standpoint, without reference to any aesthetic judgement whatsoever. The implication is that we have returned to the cultural stage of primitive societies. (The speculative fetishism of the art market itself partakes of the ritual of art's transparency.)

We find ourselves in the realm either of ultra- or of infra-aesthetics. It is pointless to try to endow our art with an aesthetic consistency or an aesthetic teleology. That would be like looking for the blue of the sky at the level of infrared and ultraviolet rays.

In this sense, therefore, inasmuch as we have access to neither the beautiful nor the ugly, and are incapable of judging, we are condemned to indifference. Beyond this indifference, however, another kind of fascination emerges, a fascination which replaces aesthetic pleasure. For, once liberated from their respective constraints, the beautiful and the ugly, in a sense, multiply: they become more beautiful than beautiful, more ugly than ugly. Thus painting currently cultivates, if not ugliness exactly – which remains an aesthetic value – then the uglier-than-ugly (the 'bad', the 'worse', kitsch), an ugliness raised to the second power because it is liberated from any relationship with its opposite. Once freed from the 'true' Mondrian, we are at liberty to 'out-Mondrian Mondrian'; freed from the true *naïfs*, we can paint in a way that is 'more *naïf* than *naïf*', and so on. And once freed from reality, we can produce the 'realer than real' – hyperrealism. It was in fact with hyperrealism and pop art that everything began, that everyday life was raised to the ironic power of photographic realism. Today this escalation has caught up every form of art, every style; and all, without discrimination, have entered the transaesthetic world of simulation.

There is a parallel to this escalation in the art market itself. Here too, because an end has been put to any deference to the law of value, to the logic of commodities, everything has become 'more expensive than expensive' – expensive, as it were, squared. Prices are exorbitant – the bidding has gone through the roof. Just as the abandonment of all aesthetic ground rules provokes a kind of brush fire of aesthetic values, so the loss of all reference to the laws of exchange means that the market hurtles into unrestrained speculation.

The frenzy, the folly, the sheer excess are the same. The promotional ignition of art is directly linked to the impossibility of all aesthetic evaluation. In the absence of value judgements, value goes up in flames. And it goes up in a sort of ecstasy.

There are two art markets today. One is still regulated by a hierarchy of values, even if these are already of a speculative kind. The other resembles nothing so much as floating and uncontrollable capital in the financial market: it is pure speculation, movement for movement's sake, with no apparent purpose other than to defy the law of value. This second art market has much in common with poker or potlatch – it is a kind of space opera in the hyperspace of value. Should we be scandalized? No. There is nothing immoral here. Just as present-day art is beyond beautiful and ugly, the market, for its part, is beyond good and evil.

TRANSSEXUALITY

The sexual body has now been assigned a kind of artificial fate. This fate is transsexuality – 'transsexual' not in any anatomical sense, but rather in the more general sense of transvestitism, of playing with the commutability of the signs of sex – and of playing, in contrast to the former manner of playing on sexual difference, on sexual indifference: on lack of differentiation between the sexual poles, and on indifference to sex *qua* pleasure. Sexuality is underpinned by pleasure, by *jouissance* (the leitmotiv of sexual liberation); transsexuality is underpinned by artifice – be it the artifice of actually changing sex or the artifice of the transvestite who plays with the sartorial, morphological or gestural signs of sex. But whether the operation in question is surgical or semio-urgical, whether it involves organs or signs, we are in any case concerned with replacement parts, and since today the body is fated to become a prosthesis, it is logical enough that our model of sexuality should have become transsexuality, and that transsexuality should have everywhere become the locus of seduction.

We are all transsexuals, just as we are biological mutants *in potentia*. This is not a biological issue, however: we are all transsexuals *symbolically*.

Take La Cicciolina. Is there any more marvellous incarnation of sex – of sex in pornographic innocence? La Cicciolina has been contrasted with Madonna, virgin fruit of the aerobic sphere, product of a glacial aesthetic, devoid of all charm and all sensuality – a numbed android who by virtue of this very fact was perfect raw material for a synthetic idol. But is not La Cicciolina too a transsexual? Her long platinum hair, her customized breasts, her realer-than-real curves worthy of an inflatable doll, her lyophilic eroticism borrowed from a comic-strip or science-fiction world, and above all the hyperbole of her (never perverse or libertine) sexual discourse – all conspire to offer a ready-made and total sinfulness; La Cicciolina is the ideal woman of a telephone chat-line complete with a carnivorous erotic ideology that no modern woman could possibly espouse – except, that is, for a transsexual, or a transvestite, these being the only people left who live through the signs of an overdrawn, rapacious sexuality. La Cicciolina, as carnal ectoplasm, is here very close to Madonna's artificial nitroglycerine or to Michael Jackson's androgynous and Frankensteinian appeal. All of them are mutants, transvestites, genetically baroque beings whose erotic look conceals their generic lack of specificity. They are all 'gender-benders' – all turncoats of sex.

Consider Michael Jackson, for example. Michael Jackson is a solitary mutant, a precursor of a hybridization that is perfect because it is universal – the race to end all races. Today's young people have no problem with a miscegenated society: they already inhabit such a universe, and Michael Jackson fore-shadows what they see as an ideal future. Add to this the fact that Michael has had his face lifted, his hair straightened, his skin lightened – in short, he has been reconstructed with the greatest attention to detail. This is what makes him such an innocent and pure child – the artificial hermaphrodite of the fable, better able even than Christ to reign over the world and reconcile its contradictions; better than a child–god because he is child–prosthesis, an embryo of all those dreamt-of mutations that will deliver us from race and from sex.

One might also consider the transvestites of the aesthetic sphere – of whom Andy Warhol must surely be the emblematic figure. Like Michael Jackson, Andy Warhol is a solitary mutant – a precursor, for his part, of a perfect and universal hybridization of art, of a new aesthetic to end all aesthetics. Like Jackson, he is a perfectly artificial personality: he too is innocent and pure, an androgyne of the new generation, a sort of mystical prosthesis or artificial machine capable, thanks to its perfection, of releasing us at one blow from the grip of both sex and aesthetics. When Warhol says: all works are beautiful – I don't have to choose between them because all contemporary works are equivalent; when he says: art is everywhere, therefore it no longer exists, everyone is a genius, the world as it is, in its very banality, is inhabited by genius – nobody is ready to believe him. Yet his is in fact an accurate description of the shape of the modern aesthetic, an aesthetic of radical agnosticism.

We are all agnostics, transvestites of art or of sex. None of us has either aesthetic or sexual convictions any longer – yet we all profess to have them.

The myth of sexual liberation is still alive and well under many forms in the real world, but at the level of the imaginary it is the transsexual myth, with its androgynous and hermaphroditic variants, that holds sway. After the orgy, then, a masked ball. After the demise of desire, a pell-mell diffusion of erotic simulacra in every guise, of transsexual kitsch in all its glory. A postmodern pornography, if you will, where sexuality is lost in the theatrical excess of its ambiguity. Things have certainly changed since the days when sexuality and politics constituted a single subversive project: if La Cicciolina can now be elected to the Italian Parliament, this is precisely because the transsexual and the transpolitical have combined within the same ironic indifference. This performance, unthinkable just a few short years ago, testifies to the fact that it is not just sexual culture but the whole of political culture that has now come beneath the banner of transvestitism.

This strategy for exorcizing the body by means of the signs of sex, for conjuring away desire through the overkill of its staging, is a good deal more efficient than good old repression founded on taboo. But where this new system really differs from the old is that one cannot see at all who stands to gain from it – for everyone suffers from it equally. The rule of transvestitism has become the very basis of our behaviour, even in our own search for identity and difference. We no longer have time to search for an identity for ourselves in the archives, in a memory, in a project or a future. Instead we are supposed to have an instant memory to which we can plug in directly for immediate access to a kind of public-relations identity. What is sought today is not so much health, which is an organic equilibrium, as an ephemeral, hygienic and promotional radiance from the body – much more a performance than an ideal state. In terms of fashion and appearances, what we seek is less beauty or attractiveness than the right *look*.

Everyone seeks their *look*. Since it is no longer possible to base any claim on one's own existence, there is nothing for it but to perform an *appearing act* without concerning oneself with *being* – or even with *being seen*. So it is not: I exist, I am here! but rather: I am visible, I am an image – look! look! This is not even narcissism, merely an extraversion without depth, a sort of self-promoting ingenuousness whereby everyone becomes the manager of their own appearance.

The 'look' is a sort of minimal low-definition image, like a video image – or what McLuhan would call a tactile image, an image which draws neither attention nor admiration – as fashion still does – but is no more than a special effect, with no particular significance. The look is no longer a function of fashion – it is a form of fashion that has been overtaken. It no longer even appeals to a logic of distinction, it is no longer founded on an interplay of differences: it *plays at difference without believing in it*. It is, in fact, indifference. Being oneself has become a transient performance with no sequel, a disabused mannerism in a world without manners.

The triumph of the transsexual and of transvestitism casts a strange light, retrospectively, upon the sexual liberation espoused by an earlier generation. It now appears that this liberation – which, according to its own discourse, meant the bursting forth of the body's full erotic force, a process especially favourable to the principles of femininity and of sexual pleasure – may actually have been no more than an intermediate phase on the way to the confusion of categories that we have been discussing. The sexual revolution may thus turn out to have been just a stage in the genesis of transsexuality. What is at issue here, fundamentally, is the problematic fate of all revolutions.

The cybernetic revolution, in view of the equivalence of brain and computer, places humanity before the crucial question 'Am I a man or a machine?' The genetic revolution that is taking place at the moment raises the question 'Am I a man or just a potential clone?' The sexual revolution, by liberating all the potentialities of desire, raises another fundamental question, 'Am I a man or a woman?' (If it has done nothing else, psychoanalysis has certainly added its weight to this principle of sexual uncertainty.) As for the political and social revolution, the prototype for all the others, it will turn out to have led man by an implacable logic – having offered him his own freedom, his own free will – to ask himself where his own will lies, what he wants in his heart of hearts, and what he is entitled to expect from himself. To these questions there are no answers. Such is the paradoxical outcome of every revolution: revolution opens the door to indeterminacy, anxiety and confusion. Once the orgy was over, liberation was seen to have left everyone looking for their generic and sexual identity – and with fewer and fewer answers available, in view of the traffic in signs and the multiplicity of pleasures on offer. That is how we became transsexuals – just as we became transpoliticals: in other words, politically indifferent and undifferentiated beings, androgynous and her-maphroditic – for by this time we had embraced, digested and rejected the most contradictory ideologies, and were left wearing only their masks: we had become, in our own heads – and perhaps unbeknownst to ourselves – transvestites of the political realm.

TRANSECONOMICS

The interesting thing about the Wall Street crash of 1987 was the uncertainty about it. Was it a true catastrophe? And is real catastrophe to be expected in the future? Answer: there cannot be a real catastrophe because we live under the sign of *virtual* catastrophe.

What did become crystal clear on this occasion was the discrepancy between the economy as we imagine it to be and the economy as it really is. It is this very discrepancy that protects us from a real catastrophe of the productive economies.

Is it a good thing or a bad thing? There is a clear parallel here with the discrepancy between orbital war and local wars. Local wars are carried on everywhere, but nuclear war never breaks out. If there were no clear divide between the two, nuclear showdown would have occurred long ago. We live in the shadow of all kinds of 'bombs' that don't go off – virtual catastrophes that never take place: an international stock-exchange and financial crash, nuclear showdown, the Third World debt, the population time bomb . . . Of course, one might say that all these bombs will indeed explode sooner or later – just as

California is bound, sometime in the next fifty years, to sink into the Pacific for seismic reasons. But the simple fact is that we experience no such explosions. Our only reality is an unchecked orbital whirl of capital which, when it does crash, causes no substantial disequilibrium in real economies (in sharp contrast to the crisis of 1929, when the rift between imaginary and real economies was far narrower). The reason, no doubt, is that the realm of mobile and speculative capital has achieved so great an autonomy that even its cataclysms leave no traces.

Where they do leave a mark – and a murderously destructive one – is in economic theory itself, which has been completely disarmed by the disintegration of its object of study. The same goes for the theorists of war. They too have a bomb that doesn't go off, while war itself has become two different things: on the one hand a total but virtual war, an orbital war; on the other hand a multiplicity of real wars at ground level. The two are quite different in scale, and do not obey the same rules – much like the virtual and the real economies. We simply have to get used to this split, to a world dominated by this distortion. Of course, there really was a crisis in 1929, and Hiroshima really happened, so both financial crashes and nuclear bombs have had their respective moments of truth. But there has been no series of increasingly serious crashes (as Marx predicted), nor has war gone from one nuclear showdown to the next. In each case, there was one event – and that was that. The sequel has been something else entirely: both big financial capital and the means of destruction have been 'hyper-realized' – and both are now in orbit above our heads on courses which not only escape our control but, by the same token, escape from reality itself. War hyper-realized and money hyper-realized circulate alike in a space which is inaccessible – but which consequently leaves the world just as it is. The upshot is that our (real) economies continue to produce, even though the slightest logical consequence of the fluctuations occurring in our imagined economy would have sufficed to destroy them utterly (we should not forget that the total volume of trade currently represents a mere forty-fifth of the total movement of capital). Similarly, the world continues to exist even though the detonation of a thousandth part of the available nuclear explosives would have reduced it to nothing. The Third World and the developed world continue to survive, even though the most minimal gesture in the direction of auditing the one's debt to the other would effectively bring all trade to a halt. Furthermore, this debt has itself already begun to go into orbit, circulating from one bank to another, or from one country to another, as it is bought and sold – indeed, this, no doubt, is how we will end up forgetting about it altogether, and sending it definitively into orbit along with nuclear waste and not a few other things. An ever-revolving debt, a lack of capital that circulates, a negative wealth that will doubtless one day be quoted on the Stock Exchange in its own right: true marvels!

When a debt becomes too cumbersome, then, it is banished to a virtual space where it resembles a deep-frozen catastrophe in orbit. Debt becomes a satellite of Earth, just like war, and just like the millions of dollars' worth of floating capital now conglomerated into a satellite tirelessly circling us. And surely this is for the best. Just so long as such satellites keep circulating – and even if they explode out in space (like the 'lost' billions of the 1987 crash) – the world is not affected by them, which is the best possible outcome. For the suggestion that the imaginary economy and the real one might one day be reconciled is a utopian one: those billions of floating dollars are untranslatable into real economic terms – and that is just as well, because if, *per mirabile*, they could be reinjected into productive economies, the result, for once, would be a true catastrophe. Likewise the virtuality of war is best left in orbit – for it is from there that it protects us: in its most abstract form, in its present monstrous excentricity, nuclear capability is our best protection. We may as well accustom ourselves to living in the shadow of such excrescences as the orbital bomb, financial speculation, worldwide debt and overpopulation (for which last no orbital solution has yet been found, though there is still hope). Such as they are, in their excessiveness, in their very hyper-reality, they are self-exorcizing, and they leave the world in a sense intact, freed from the threat of its double.

Victor Segalen observed that from the moment we became certain that the Earth was a sphere, travel ceased to exist – for to leave any point on the surface of a sphere is also necessarily to begin the return to that same point. Linearity on a sphere has a curve to it – the curve of monotony. From the moment when the first astronauts began circling Earth, we each began secretly circling round ourselves. The orbital era is here. Space is a part of it, but its expression *par excellence* is television, as well as a good few other things, among them the rondo of the molecular spirals of DNA within the recesses of our cells. The first orbital space flights marked the completion of the process of globalization, but also the moment when progress itself became circular, when the human universe was reduced to a vast orbital machine. What Segalen called 'tourism' could really begin: the perpetual tourism of people who no longer undertake voyages in the true sense, but simply go round and round in circles within their circumscribed territory. Exoticism was now dead and buried.

But Segalen's remark has a wider application. It is not just travel – that is to say, the way in which the Earth is imagined – and not just the physics and metaphysics of transcendence and discovery that have been erased in favour of mere circulation, for everything which once aspired to transcendence, to discovery, to the infinite, has subtly altered its aim so that it can go into orbit: learning, technology, knowledge, having lost any transcendent aspect to their projects, have begun planning orbital trajectories for themselves. 'Information' is orbital, for example – a form of knowledge which will never again go beyond itself, never again achieve transcendence or self-reflection in its aspiration towards the infinite; yet which, for all that, never sets its feet on the ground, for it has no true purchase on, nor referent in, reality. Information circulates, moves around, makes its circuits (which are sometimes perfectly useless – but that is the whole point: the question of usefulness cannot be raised) – and with each spiral, each revolution, it accumulates. Television is an image which no longer dreams, no longer imagines, but nevertheless has nothing whatsoever to do with reality. An orbital circuit. The nuclear bomb, whether actually satellite-borne or not, is also orbital: its trajectory must inevitably remain an obsession for the planet, yet at the same time it is not supposed to come back down to earth: this is no longer a finite bomb – nor a bomb that will even (we must hope!) achieve its end; it is simply there, in its orbit, and the terror it evokes – or at any rate, its power of dissuasion – is enough. It no longer even fills our dreams with terror: destruction is unimaginable. The bomb is simply there, in orbit, hanging over us, revolving for ever and ever. The same is true of Eurodollars, and of the massive quantities of floating currency . . . Everything tends to become a satellite – even our brains may be said to be outside us now, floating around us in the countless Hertzian ramifications of waves and circuits.

This is not science fiction, merely a generalization of McLuhan's theory of the 'extensions of man'. Every aspect of human beings – their bodies in their biological, mental, muscular or cerebral manifestations – now floats free in the shape of mechanical or computer-aided replacement parts. McLuhan, however, conceives of all this as a positive expansion – as the universalization of man – through media. This is a very sanguine view. The fact is that all the functions of man's body, so far from gravitating around him in *concentric* order, have become satellites ordered *excentrically* with respect to him. They have gone into orbit on their own account; consequently it is man himself, in view of this orbital extraversion of his own functions, his own technologies, who is now in a position of ex-orbitation and ex-centricity. *Vis-à-vis* the satellites that he has created and put into orbit, it is man with his planet Earth, with his territory, with his body, who is now the satellite. Once transcendent, he has become exorbitate.

It is not just the functions of man's body which, by becoming satellites, make man himself into a satellite. All those functions of our societies – notably the higher ones – which break off and go into orbit, contribute to the process. Loan, finance, the technosphere, communications – all have become satellites in an inaccessible space and left everything else to go to rack and ruin. Whatever fails to achieve orbital power is left in a state of abandonment which is permanent, since there is now no way out of it via some kind of transcendence.

We are in the age of weightlessness. It is as though our model were a niche in space whose kinetic energy cancels out our Earth's gravity. The centrifugal force of our proliferating technologies has stripped us of all weight and transferred us into an empty freedom of movement. Freed of all density, all gravity, we are being dragged into an orbital motion which threatens to become perpetual.

We are now governed not so much by growth as by growths. Ours is a society founded on proliferation, on growth which continues even though it cannot be measured against any clear goals. An excrescential society whose development is uncontrollable, occurring without regard for self-definition, where the accumulation of effects goes hand in hand with the disappearance of causes. The upshot is gross systemic congestion and malfunction caused by hypertelia – by an excess of functional imperatives, by a sort of saturation. There is no better analogy here than the metastatic process in cancer: a loss of the body's organic ground rules such that a given group of cells is able to deploy its incoercible and murderous vitality, to defy genetic programming and to proliferate endlessly.

This process is not a *critical* one: crisis is always a matter of causality, of an imbalance between cause and effect to which a solution will be found (or not) by attending to causes. In our case, by contrast, it is the causes themselves that are tending to disappear, tending to become indecipherable, and giving way to an intensification of processes operating in a void.

So long as there is a dysfunction in a system, a departure from known laws governing its operation, there is always the prospect of transcending the problem. But when a system rides roughshod over its own basic assumptions, supersedes its own ends, so that no remedy can be found, then we are contemplating not crisis but catastrophe. Deficiency is never a complete disaster, but saturation is fatal, for it produces a sort of tetanized inertia.

The striking thing about all present-day systems is their bloatedness: the means we have devised for handling data – communication, record-keeping, storage, production and destruction – are all in a condition of 'demonic pregnancy' (to borrow Susan Sontag's description of cancer). So lethargic are they, indeed, that they will assuredly never again serve a useful purpose. It is not we that have put an end to use-value – rather, the system itself has eliminated it through surplus production. So many things have been produced and accumulated that they can never possibly all be put to use (certainly not a bad thing in the case of nuclear weapons). So many messages and signals are produced and disseminated that they can never possibly all be read. A good thing for us too – for even with the tiny portion that we do manage to absorb, we are in a state of permanent electrocution.

There is something particularly nauseating about this prodigious uselessness, about a proliferating yet hypertrophied world which cannot give birth to anything. So many reports, archives, documents – and not a single idea generated; so many plans, programmes, decisions – and not a single event precipitated; so many sophisticated weapons produced – and no war declared!

This saturation goes way beyond the surplus that Bataille spoke of; all societies have found some way to dispose of that through useless or sumptuous expense. There is no possible way for us to spend all that has been accumulated – all we have in prospect is a slow or brutal decompensation, with each factor of acceleration serving to create inertia, bringing us closer to absolute inertia. What we call crisis is in fact a foreshadowing of this absolute inertia.

We confront a paradoxical process, then, whose duality – tetanization and inertia, acceleration in a void, overheated production with no attendant social gains or aims – is a reflection of the two phenomena conventionally attributed to the crisis: inflation and unemployment.

Traditionally, inflation and unemployment are variables in the equation of growth. At this level, however, there is really no question of crisis: these phenomena are anomic in character, and anomie is merely the shadow cast by an organic solidarity. What is worrying, by contrast, is *anomaly*. The anomalous is not a clear symptom but, rather, a strange sign of failure, of the infraction of a rule which is secret – or which, at any rate, we know nothing about. Perhaps an excess of goals is the culprit – we simply do not know. Something escapes us, and we are escaping from ourselves, or losing ourselves, as part of an irreversible process; we have now passed some point of no return, the point where the contradictoriness of things ended, and we find ourselves, still alive, in a universe of non-contradiction, of enthusiasm, of ecstasy – of stupor in the face of a process which, for all its irreversibility, is bereft of meaning.

There is something much more shattering than inflation, however, and that is the mass of floating money whirling about the Earth in an orbital rondo. Money is now the only genuine artificial satellite. A pure artifact, it enjoys a truly astral mobility; and it is instantaneously convertible. Money has now found its proper place, a place far more wondrous than the stock exchange: the orbit in which it rises and sets like some artificial sun.

Unemployment, too, has taken on new meaning. It is no longer a strategy of capital (the reserve army of labour). It is no longer a critical factor in the play of social relationships – if it were, since the danger level was passed long ago, it would necessarily have sparked unprecedented upheavals. What is unemployment today? It too is a sort of artificial satellite, a satellite of inertia, a mass with a charge of electricity that cannot even be described as a negative charge, for it is static: I refer to that increasingly large portion of society that is deep-frozen. Beneath the accelerating pace of the circuits and systems of exchange, beneath all the frenzied activity, there is something in us – in each of us – that slows down to the point where it fades out of circulation. This is the inertia point around which the whole of society eventually begins to gravitate. It is as though the two poles of our world had been brought into contact, short-circuiting in such a way that they simultaneously hyperstimulate and enervate potential energies. This is no longer a crisis, but a fatal development – a catastrophe in slow motion.

Not the least of paradoxes, given this context, is to see the economy returning triumphantly to the agenda – though whether we can properly speak of 'economy' here is questionable. Certainly this glaring reality of today cannot have the meaning it had in the classical or Marxist accounts. Its motor is neither the infrastructure nor the superstructure of material production, but rather the *destructuring* of value, the destabilization of real markets and economies and the victory of an economy unencumbered by ideologies, by social science, by history – an economy freed from 'Economics' and given over to pure speculation; a virtual economy emancipated from real economies (not emancipated *in reality*, of course: we are talking about *virtuality* – but that is the point, too: today, power lies not in the real but in the virtual); and an economy which is *viral*, and which thus connects with all other viral processes. If the economic sphere has once more become an exemplary theatre of our present reality, it has done so as the locus of special effects, of unforeseeable events, of an irrational interplay of forces.

Along with Marx, we too dreamt of the end of Political Economy – of the abolition of classes and the advent of a transparent social realm in accordance with the ineluctable logic of Capital. And then we dreamt of the end of the economy in terms of a disavowal of its basic tenets – a disavowal that threw out the Marxist critique into the bargain: on this view, primacy was accorded neither to the economic nor to the political – the economy was simply ushered out as a mere epiphenomenon, vanquished by its simulacrum of itself, and by a superior logic.

Today we no longer even need to dream: Political Economy is coming to an end before our eyes, metamorphosing into a transeconomics of speculation which merely *plays* at obeying the old logic (the law of value, the laws of the market, production, surplus-value, all the classical laws of capital) and therefore no longer has anything economic or political about it. A game and nothing but a game, with floating and arbitrary rules: a game of catastrophe.

So Political Economy will indeed soon have come to an end – though not at all in the way we once envisaged: rather, through the exacerbation of its own logic to the point of self-parody.

Speculation is not surplus-value, it is a sort of ecstasy of value, utterly detached from production and its real conditions: a pure, empty form, the purged *form* of value operating on nothing but its own revolving motion, its own orbital circulation. The self-destabilization of Political Economy is thus what puts paid, in monstrous and somehow ironic fashion, to all possible alternatives. What possible riposte could there be to such extravagance, which effectively co-opts the energy of poker, of potlatch, of the 'accursed share', and in a way opens the door to Political Economy's aesthetic and delusional stage? This unexpected demise, this phase transition, this wild bull market, is fundamentally far more original than all our old political utopias.

SUPERCONDUCTIVE
EVENTS

We are witnessing the rise – the simultaneous rise – of terrorism as a transpolitical form, of AIDS and cancer as forms of pathology, of transsexuality and transvestitism as forms that are sexual and, in a general way, aesthetic. These forms, and these forms alone, are what fascinate us today. Nobody is now the slightest bit interested in sexual liberation, political discussion, organic illnesses, or even conventional warfare (a fact for which we may be grateful so far as war is concerned: a good many wars will not have taken place merely because they held no interest for anyone). Our true phantasies lie elsewhere – specifically, they focus on the three above-mentioned forms, each of which arises from the skewing of a basic operating principle and the confusion that results from this. These forms, terrorism, transvestitism, and cancer, all reflect excesses – on the political, sexual and genetic levels respectively; they also reflect deficiencies in – and the consequent collapse of – the codes of the political, sexual and genetic realms.

All these forms are viral – fascinating, indiscriminate – and their virulence is reinforced by their images, for the modern media have a viral force of their own, and their virulence is contagious. Ours is a culture in which bodies and minds are irradiated by signals and images; little wonder, then, that for all its marvels this culture also produces the most murderous viruses. The nuclearization of our bodies began with Hiroshima, but it continues endemically, incessantly, in the shape of our irradiation by media, signs, programs, networks.

We are subject to a veritable bombardment by 'superconductive' events – by the kind of untimely intercontinental whirlwinds which no longer affect just states, individuals or institutions, but rather entire transversal structures: sex, money, information, communications, etc.

This is not to say that AIDS, financial crashes, computer viruses and terrorism are somehow interchangeable, merely that they do have a family resemblance. Thus AIDS is certainly a sort of crash in sexual values, while computers played a 'virulent' role in the Wall Street crash of 1987; meanwhile computers are themselves at risk of viral infection – of 'crashes' in the information market. Moreover, infection is no longer confined within a given system but can leap from one system to another. All these tendencies revolve around one generic scenario – that of catastrophe. Of course, the signs of trouble have long been apparent: AIDS has long since entered its endemic stage; the threat of financial crisis has been ever present since the celebrated precedent of 1929; and computer pirates and electronic accidents have already been with us for over twenty years. But the conjunction of all these endemic forms and their almost simultaneous transition to a state of full-blown anomaly have brought about a unique state of affairs. Their respective effects are not necessarily of the same order in the popular consciousness: AIDS can, of course, be experienced as a genuine catastrophe; the stock-market crash seems, by contrast, like a kind of *playing at* catastrophe; as for computer viruses, for all their dramatic consequences there is poetic justice here, and when a sudden epidemic strikes the computer world, a common and not incomprehensible reaction (except among computer professionals) is hilarity.

The general effect is reinforced by other factors too. Art, which is everywhere susceptible to fraud, to copying, to simulation, and at the same time to the raving hyperbole of the art market, epitomizes a body irradiated by lucre. Consider terrorism. Nothing more closely resembles the chain reaction of terrorism in our irradiated societies than the chain reactions associated with AIDS, with Wall Street raiders or with software saboteurs. (And, by the way, what are these societies irradiated *by*? By the superfusion of happiness and security, information and communication? By the disintegration of symbolic nexuses, fundamental rules, or social contracts? It is anybody's guess.) The contagiousness of terrorism, its fascination, is every bit as enigmatic as the contagiousness of these other phenomena. When a programmer introduces a 'soft bomb' into his software and uses his resultant destructive power as a threat, is he not in effect taking the program and all its applications hostage? Likewise, are corporate raiders not taking and holding businesses hostage when they speculate on their demise or resurrection in the stock market? All these phenomena operate on the same model as terrorism (hostages have a quoted price just like shares or pictures), but one might just as easily explain terrorism in terms of a parallel with AIDS, with computer viruses, or with public stock offerings. No phenomenon in this constellation of phenomena has priority *vis-à-vis* the others. (Consider the recent release of an informational diskette on AIDS which was itself infected by a computer virus.)

Science fiction? Hardly. In the spheres of information and communication, too, the value of the message is purely that of its circulation, its passage from one image to another, one screen to another. We all get pleasure from this new centrifugal value – from the stock exchange, the art market or corporate raiders as spectacle. We all enjoy these things as spectacular breathing spaces under capitalism, as by-products of capital's aesthetic delusions. And we delight in the system's secret pathology, in the viruses that batten on its splendid machinery and send it haywire. In fact, however, the viruses are part and parcel of the hyperlogical consistency of our systems; they follow all the pathways of those systems, and even open up new ones (computer viruses explore possibilities of networks that were never anticipated by those networks' designers). Electronic viruses are an expression of the murderous transparency of information on a world scale. AIDS is the product of the murderous transparency of sex affecting entire human groups. Stock-market crashes reflect the murderous transparency of economies with respect to one another and the astounding circulation of values that is the very basis of the liberation of production and exchange. Once 'liberated', all these processes undergo a kind of superfusion much like nuclear superfusion, which is in fact their prototype. This superfusion of chains of events is not the least of the charms of our time.

Nor, if the succession of events exercises a charm, is unpredictability by any means the least part of it. When a forecast is made, no matter what it may be, it is always tempting to prove it wrong. Events themselves often help us out in this regard. There are overpredicted events, for instance, that obligingly decline to occur; and then there are the exactly opposite kind – those which occur without forewarning. It behoves us to bank on such conjunctural surprises – such 'backdraughts'. We must bet on the *Witz* of events them-selves. If we lose, at least we shall have had the satisfaction of defying the objective idiocy of the probabilities. This obligation is a vital function – part of our collective genetic heritage. Indeed, this is the only genuine function of the intellect: to embrace contradictions, to exercise irony, to take the opposite tack, to exploit rifts and reversibility – even to fly in the face of the lawful and the factual. If the intellectuals of today seem to have run out of things to say, this is because they have failed to assume this ironic function, confining themselves within the limits of their moral, political or philosophical consciousness despite the fact that the rules have changed, that all irony, all radical criticism now belongs exclusively to the haphazard, the viral, the catastrophic – to accidental or system-led reversals. Such are the new rules of the game – such is the new principle of uncertainty that now holds sway over all. The operation of this principle is a source of intense intellectual satisfaction (no doubt even of *spiritual* satisfaction). Think of the computer-virus story: something in us leaps with joy when we hear of an event of this kind. It is not that we have a perverse love of catastrophe – this is not the glee of the doomsayer proved right. No, it is that there is a suggestion of fatality here – and fatality always provokes a certain elation in us.

An outcome is fatal when the same sign presides over both the advent of something and its demise, when the same star that gave hope leads eventually to disaster, or (as in the case of computer viruses) when the logic that informs a system's expansion then proceeds to devastate it. The fatal in this sense is the opposite of the accidental. The accidental is peripheral to a system, whereas fatality is immanent. (Not that fatality always means disaster: the unforesee-able harvest of fate may also be enchantment.) It is quite conceivable that something of this diabolic principle may be found at work – albeit in homeo-pathically small doses – even in the slight anomalies or tiny malfunctions that affect our statistical universe.

Can this *Witz* of events be counted on to come into play every time? Of course not. But the point is precisely that one can never be sure of what is plainly evident. When the truth is incontestable, it loses credibility on that account; even science is liable to be caught short. There is nothing academic about the thesis that statistical truths can always be refuted. On the contrary, it is a hope put about by the evil genie of a quintessentially popular wisdom.

Once upon a time there was much talk of the apathy of the masses. Their silence was the crucial fact for an earlier generation. Today, however, the masses act not by deflection but by infection, tainting opinion polls and forecasts with their multifarious phantasies. Their abstention and their silence are no longer determining factors (that stage was still nihilistic); what counts now is their use of the cogs in the workings of uncertainty. Where the masses once sported with their voluntary servitude, they now sport with their invo-luntary incertitude. Unbeknownst to the experts who scrutinize them and the manipulators who believe they can influence them, they have grasped the fact that politics is virtually dead, and that they now have a new game to play, just as exciting as the ups and downs of the stock market. This game enables them to make audiences, charismas, levels of prestige and the market prices of images dance up and down with an intolerable facility. The masses had been deliberately demoralized and de-ideologized in order that they might become the live prey of probability theory, but now it is they who destabilize all images and play games with political truth. They are merely playing as they have been taught to play, speculating on the Bourse of statistics and images. This speculation is total, and immoral, just like that of the financial speculators. In the face of the idiotic certainty and inexorable banality of numbers, the masses are an incarnation, on the margins, of the principle of uncertainty in the sociological sphere. As the powers-that-be strive to organize their statistical order (and the social order is now a statistical order), so it falls to the masses to look, in clandestine fashion, to the interests of statistical disorder.

It is from this viral, diabolic, ironic and reversible posture of the masses that we are perhaps entitled to expect some unprecedented development – some *Witz* of the events themselves.

This society now produces only ill-defined events whose ultimate clarification is unlikely. In earlier times an event was something that happened – now it is something that is designed to happen. It occurs, therefore, as a virtual artifact, as a reflection of pre-existing media-defined forms.

The virus that wreaked havoc for five hours in the US scientific and military computer network *may have been* just a test (as Paul Virilio has suggested) – an experiment carried out by American military intelligence itself: an event at once stage-managed and simulated. Either a true accident, then, bearing witness to the effective virulence of such viruses, or a total simulation, showing that the most effective strategy today is calculated destabilization and deception. The verdict is not yet in. Even if the hypothesis of an experimental simulation were to be confirmed, moreover, this would in no way guarantee that the process involved was under control. A test virus can always turn into a killer virus. No one can control chain reactions of this kind, and any simulated accident is potentially an accident of simulation. What is more, we know that any natural accident or catastrophe may be claimed as a terrorist act, and vice versa. There is no limit here to the hyperbole of hypotheses.

It is in this respect, in fact, that the whole system is globally terroristic. A greater terror than the terror of violence and accident is the terror of uncertainty and dissuasion. A few years ago a group that had staged a mock hold-up was penalized more heavily than they would have been for an actual robbery: the fact is that attacks on the reality principle itself constitute a graver offence than real-life violence.

What is constant is an immense uncertainty, an uncertainty which lies at the core of the present operational euphoria. The natural sciences were the first to describe a panic situation of this kind: it is the disappearance of the respective positions of subject and object at the experimental interface that has given rise to a definitive state of uncertainty about the reality of the object and the (objective) reality of knowledge. Science itself seems to have fallen under the sway of its strange attractors. But the same goes for the economy, whose resurrection is apparently bound up with the total unpredictability that now reigns within it. Likewise the sudden expansion of data-handling techniques is seemingly tied to the indefiniteness of the knowledge with which these techniques are designed to deal.

Are all techniques of this kind actively engaged with the real world? It is extremely doubtful. The aim of science and technology would seem to be much more that of presenting us with a definitively unreal world, beyond all criteria of truth and reality. The revolution of our time is the uncertainty revolution.

We are not ready to accept this. Paradoxically, however, we attempt to escape from uncertainty by relying even more on information and communications systems, so merely aggravating the uncertainty itself. This is a forward flight: the pursuit race of technology and its perverse effects, of man and his clones, around a track in the form of a Moebius strip, has only just begun.

OPERATIONAL WHITEWASH

The uncertainty to which we are subject results, paradoxically, from an excess of positivity, from an ineluctable drop in the level of negativity. A kind of leukaemia has taken hold of our societies – a kind of dissolution of negativity in a perfused euphoria. Neither the French Revolution, nor the philosophy of the Enlightenment, nor critical utopianism has found its fulfilment through the supersession of contradictions, and if the problems they addressed have been solved, this has been achieved by casting off the negative, by disseminating the energies of everything condemned by society within a simulation entirely given over to positivity and factitiousness, by instituting a definitively transparent state of affairs. Ours is rather like the situation of the man who has lost his shadow: either he has become transparent, and the light passes right through him or, alternatively, he is lit from all angles, overexposed and defenceless against all sources of light. We are similarly exposed on all sides to the glare of technology, images and information, without any way of refracting their rays; and we are doomed in consequence to a whitewashing of all activity – whitewashed social relations, whitewashed bodies, whitewashed memory –

in short, to a complete aseptic whiteness. Violence is whitewashed, history is whitewashed, all as part of a vast enterprise of cosmetic surgery at whose completion nothing will be left but a society for which, and individuals for whom, all violence, all negativity, are strictly forbidden. In these circumstances everything which is unable to relinquish its own identity is inevitably plunged into a realm of radical uncertainty and endless simulation.

We are under the sway of a surgical compulsion that seeks to excise negative characteristics and remodel things synthetically into ideal forms. Cosmetic surgery: a face's chance configuration, its beauty or ugliness, its distinctive traits, its negative traits – all these have to be corrected, so as to produce something more beautiful than beautiful: an ideal face, a *surgical* face. Even one's astrological sign, one's birth sign, can now be revised so as to harmonize star and lifestyle: once a utopian notion, the idea of an Institute of Zodiacal Surgery where a few appropriate manipulations would affiliate you with your chosen sign is now clearly realistic.

Even the sex to which we belong – that small portion of destiny still remaining to us, that minimum of fatality and otherness – will be changeable at will. Not to mention cosmetic surgery as applied to green spaces, to nature in general, to genes, to events, to history (e.g. the French Revolution revised and corrected – given a facelift under the banner of human rights). Everything has to become postsynchable according to criteria of optimal convenience and compatibility. This inhuman formalization of face, speech, sex, body, will and public opinion is a tendency everywhere in evidence. Every last glimmer of fate and negativity has to be expunged in favour of something resembling the smile of a corpse in a funeral home, in favour of a general redemption of signs. To this end a gigantic campaign of plastic surgery has been undertaken.

Everything has to be sacrificed to the principle that things must have an operational genesis. So far as production is concerned, it is no longer the Earth that produces, or labour that creates wealth (the famous betrothal of Earth and Labour): rather, it is Capital that *makes* the Earth and Labour *produce*. Work is no longer an action, it is an operation. Consumption no longer means the simple enjoyment of goods, it means having (someone) enjoy something – an operation modelled on, and keyed to, the differential range of sign-objects.

Communication is a matter not of speaking but of making people speak. Information involves not knowledge but making people know. The use of the construction 'make' plus infinitive [in French, the auxiliary *faire* plus infinitive – *Trans.*] indicates that these are operations, not actions. The point in advertising and propaganda is not to believe but to make people believe. 'Participation' is not an active or spontaneous social form, because it is always induced by some sort of machinery or machination: it is not acting so much as making people act (an operation resembling animation or similar techniques).

These days even *wanting* is mediated by models of the will, by forms of making people want something – by persuasion or dissuasion. Even if such categories as wishing, being able, believing, knowing, acting, desiring and enjoying still retain some meaning, they have all been monopolized, as it were, by a simple auxiliary mode. Everywhere the active verb has given way to the factitive, and actions themselves have less importance than the fact that they are produced, induced, solicited, media-ized or technicized.

There is to be no knowledge save that which results from having (people) know. No speaking save that which results from having (people) speak – i.e. from an act of communication. No more actions save those which result from an interaction – complete, if possible, with television monitor and built-in feedback. For the thing that characterizes operation, as opposed to action, is precisely that operations are necessarily regulated in the way in which they occur – otherwise, there would be no communication. Speaking – but no communication. Communication is operational or it is nothing. Information is operational or it is nothing.

All our categories have thus entered the age of the factitious: no more wanting – only getting people to want; no more doing – only getting people to do; no more *being worth* something – merely getting something to be worth something (witness advertising in general); no more knowing – only letting know; and, last but not least, not so much enjoying, not so much taking pleasure, as getting people to enjoy, getting people to take pleasure. This is the great problem of the moment: to take sexual pleasure serves no purpose – we are supposed to *give* sexual pleasure, whether to ourselves or to others. Such pleasure has become an act of communication: I am your guest, you are my guest – we exchange pleasure as part of a performative interactivity. Anyone who seeks gratification without communication is a pig. Do communication machines have orgasms? That is another story – but if we try to imagine orgasmic machines, we can do so only by reference to the model of communication machines. As a matter of fact, such orgasmic machines already exist in the shape of our own bodies – bodies coaxed into coming by the subtlest of cosmetic and pleasure-inducing technologies.

Jogging is another activity in the thrall of the performance principle. To jog is not to run but to make one's body run. Though it is based on the body's informal performance, jogging strives to exhaust and destroy the body. The 'secondary state' induced by the activity corresponds exactly to this second operation, this mechanical derailing of the body. The pleasure (or pain) of jogging has nothing to do either with sport or with the body in its fleshly reality: it is the pleasure not of pure physical exertion but of a dematerialization, of an endless functioning. The body of the jogger is like one of Tinguely's machines: ascesis and ecstasis of the performance principle. Making the body run soon gives way, moreover, to letting the body run: the body is hypnotized by its own performance and goes on running on its own, in the absence of a subject, like a somnambulistic and celibate machine. (An analogous machine

here is Jarry's *quintuplette*, on which the dead carry on pedalling by themselves.) The interminable aspect of jogging, like the interminable aspect of
psychoanalysis, is indeed endless, aimless, illusionless performance.

It can no longer be said that the goal here is 'getting into shape', which was
an ideal of the 1960s and 1970s. Fitness then was still functional: it represented
a striving for market value, for the body's sign-value, its productivity or status.
Performance, by contrast, is operational: it is orientated not towards the body's
form but towards its formula – its equation, its potentiality as a field of
operations, as something that we cause to function because, just like any
machine, it asks to be activated; because, just like any signal, it asks to be
switched on. It is just as simple as that. Hence the deep vacuousness of the
action's content. What could be vainer than all this running for the sake of
exercising the faculty of running? And still they run . . .

The same indifference to content, the same obsessional and operational,
performative and interminable aspects, also characterize the present-day use
of computers: people no more think at a computer than they run when jogging.
They have their brain function in the first activity much as they have their body
run in the second. Here too the operation is virtually endless: a head-to-head
confrontation with a computer has no more reason to come to an end than the
physical effort that jogging demands. And the kind of hypnotic pleasure
involved, the ecstatic absorption or resorption of energy – bodily energy in one
case, cerebral in the other – is identical. On the one hand, the static electricity of
skin and muscles – on the other, the static electricity of the screen.

Jogging and working at a computer may be looked upon as drugs, as
narcotics, to the extent that all drugs are directly governed by the dominant
performance principle: they get us to take pleasure, get us to dream, get us to
feel. Drugs are not artificial in the sense of inducing a secondary state distinct
from a natural state of the body; they are artificial, however, in that they

constitute a chemical prosthesis, a mental surgery of performance, a plastic surgery of perception.

It is hardly surprising that the suspicion of systematic drug use hangs over sport today. Different forms of obeisance to the performance principle can easily set up house together. Not only muscles and nerves but also neurons and cells must be made to perform. (Even bacteria will soon have an operational role.) Throwing, running, swimming and jumping have had their day: the point now is to send a satellite called 'the body' into artificial orbit. The athlete's body has become both launcher and satellite; no longer governed by an individual will gauging the effort expended with a view to self-transcendence, it is controlled by an internal microcomputer working by calculation alone.

The compulsion to operationalism gives rise to an operational paradox. It is not just that the order of the day is 'making something worth something': the fact is that it is better, if something is to be invested with value, for it to have no value to begin with; better to know nothing in order to have things known; better to produce nothing in order to have things produced; and better to have nothing to say if one seeks to communicate. All of which is part of the logic of things: as everyone knows, if you want to make people laugh, it is better not to be funny. The implications for communication and information networks are incontestable: in order for content to be conveyed as well and as quickly as possible, that content should come as close as possible to transparency and insignificance. This principle may be seen in action in the telephone relationship or in media transmissions – as also in more serious arenas. Thus *good* communication – the foundation, today, of a *good* society – implies the annihilation of its own content. (Note that even the term 'society' has lost its meaning: the only thing that is still 'social' is whatever can be manufactured as such, as 'sociality' or 'sociability' – ghastly sobriquets which perfectly express the thing to which they refer: such terms – as François George has said of 'sexuality' – put one in mind of some form of surgery.) And if good communication implies the annihilation of its own content, good data-handling implies a digital transparency of knowledge. Good advertising implies the nullity – or at least the neutralization – of the product being advertised, just as fashion implies the transparency of women and their bodies – and just as the exercise of power implies the insignificance of those who exercise it.

What if all advertising were an apologia not for a product but for advertising itself? If information referred not to events but to the promotion of information itself *qua* event? If communication were concerned not with messages but instead with the promotion of communication itself *qua* myth?

XEROX AND INFINITY

If men create intelligent machines, or fantasize about them, it is either because they secretly despair of their own intelligence or because they are in danger of succumbing to the weight of a monstrous and useless intelligence which they seek to exorcize by transferring it to machines, where they can play with it and make fun of it. By entrusting this burdensome intelligence to machines we are released from any responsibility to knowledge, much as entrusting power to politicians allows us to disdain any aspiration of our own to power.

If men dream of machines that are unique, that are endowed with genius, it is because they despair of their own uniqueness, or because they prefer to do without it – to enjoy it by proxy, so to speak, thanks to machines. What such machines offer is the spectacle of thought, and in manipulating them people devote themselves more to the spectacle of thought than to thought itself.

It is not for nothing that they are described as 'virtual', for they put thought on hold indefinitely, tying its emergence to the achievement of a complete knowledge. The act of thinking itself is thus put off for ever. Indeed, the question of thought can no more be raised than the question of the freedom of future generations, who will pass through life as we travel through the air, strapped into their seats. These Men of Artificial Intelligence will traverse their own mental space bound hand and foot to their computers. Immobile in front of his computer, Virtual Man makes love via the screen and gives lessons by means of the teleconference. He is a physical – and no doubt also a mental – cripple. That is the price he pays for being operational. Just as eyeglasses and contact lenses will arguably one day evolve into implanted prostheses for a species that has lost its sight, it is similarly to be feared that artificial intelligence and the hardware that supports it will become a mental prosthesis for a species without the capacity for thought.

Artificial intelligence is devoid of intelligence because it is devoid of artifice. True artifice is the artifice of the body in the throes of passion, the artifice of the sign in seduction, the artifice of ambivalence in gesture, the artifice of ellipsis in language, the artifice of the mask before the face, the artifice of the pithy remark that completely alters meaning. So-called intelligent machines deploy artifice only in the feeblest sense of the word, breaking linguistic, sexual or cognitive acts down into their simplest elements and digitizing them so that they can be resynthesized according to models. They can generate all the possibilities of a program or of a potential object. But artifice is in no way concerned with what *generates*, merely with what *alters*, reality. Artifice is the power of illusion. These machines have the artlessness of pure calculation, and the games they offer are based solely on commutations and combinations. In this sense they may be said to be virtuous, as well as virtual: they can never succumb to their own object; they are immune even to the seduction of their own knowledge. Their virtue resides in their transparency, their functionality, their absence of passion and artifice. Artificial Intelligence is a celibate machine.

What must always distinguish the way humans function from the way machines function, even the most intelligent of machines, is the intoxication, the sheer pleasure, that humans get from functioning. The invention of a machine that can feel pleasure is something – happily – that is still beyond human capacity. All kinds of spare parts are available to humans to help them achieve gratification, but none has yet been devised that could take pleasure in their stead. There are prostheses that can work better than humans, 'think' or move around better than humans (or in place of humans), but there is no such thing, from the point of view of technology or in terms of the media, as a replacement for human pleasure, or for the pleasure of being human. For that to exist, machines would have to have an idea of man, have to be able to invent man – but inasmuch as man has already invented *them*, it is too late for that. That is why man can always be more than he is, whereas machines can never be more than they are. Even the most intelligent among machines are just what they are – except, perhaps, when accidents or failures occur, events which might conceivably be attributed to some obscure desire on the part of the machine. Nor do machines manifest that ironical surplus or excess functioning which contributes the pleasure, or suffering, thanks to which human beings transcend their determinations – and thus come closer to their *raison d'être*. Alas for the machine, it can never transcend its own operation – which, perhaps, explains the profound melancholy of the computer. All machines are celibate.

(All the same, the recent epidemic of computer viruses does embody a striking anomaly: it is almost as though machines were able to obtain a sly pleasure by producing perverse effects. This is an ironic and fascinating turn of events. Could it be that artificial intelligence, by manifesting this viral pathology, is engaging in self-parody – and thus acceding to some sort of genuine intelligence?)

The celibacy of the machine entails the celibacy of Telecomputer Man. Thanks to his computer or word processor, Telecomputer Man offers himself the spectacle of his own brain, his own intelligence, at work. Similarly, through his chat line or his Minitel, he can offer himself the spectacle of his own phantasies, of a strictly virtual pleasure. He exorcizes both intelligence and pleasure at the interface with the machine. The Other, the interlocutor, is never really involved: the screen works much like a mirror, for the screen itself as locus of the interface is the prime concern. An interactive screen transforms the process of relating into a process of commutation between One and the Same. The secret of the interface is that the Other here is virtually the Same: otherness is surreptitiously conjured away by the machine. The most probable scenario of communication here is that Minitel users gravitate from the screen to telephone conversations, thence to face-to-face meetings, and . . . then what? Well, it's 'let's phone each other', and, finally, back to the Minitel – which is, after all, more erotic because it is at once both esoteric and transparent. This is communication in its purest form, for there is no intimacy here except with the screen, and with an electronic text that is no more than a design filigreed onto life. A new Plato's retreat whence to observe shadow-forms of bodily pleasure filing past. Why speak to one another, when it is so simple to communicate?

We lived once in a world where the realm of the imaginary was governed by the mirror, by dividing one into two, by theatre, by otherness and alienation. Today that realm is the realm of the screen, of interfaces and duplication, of contiguity and networks. All our machines are screens, and the interactivity of humans has been replaced by the interactivity of screens. Nothing inscribed on these screens is ever intended to be deciphered in any depth: rather, it is supposed to be explored instantaneously, in an abreaction immediate to meaning, a short-circuiting of the poles of representation.

Reading a screenful of information is quite a different thing from *looking*. It is a digital form of exploration in which the eye moves along an endless broken line. The relationship to the interlocutor in communication, like the relationship to knowledge in data-handling, is similar: tactile and exploratory. A computer-generated voice, even a voice over the telephone, is a tactile voice, neutral and functional. It is no longer in fact exactly a voice, any more than looking at a screen is exactly looking. The whole paradigm of the sensory has changed. The tactility here is not the organic sense of touch: it implies merely an epidermal contiguity of eye and image, the collapse of the aesthetic distance involved in looking. We draw ever closer to the surface of the screen; our gaze is, as it were, strewn across the image. We no longer have the spectator's distance from the stage – all theatrical conventions are gone. That we fall so easily into the screen's coma of the imagination is due to the fact that the screen presents a perpetual void that we are invited to fill. Proxemics of images: promiscuity of images: tactile pornography of images. Yet the image is always light years away. It is invariably a tele-image – an image located at a very special kind of distance which can only be described as *unbridgeable by the body*. The body can cross the distance that separates it from language, from the stage, or from the mirror – this is what keeps it human and allows it to partake in exchange. But the screen is merely virtual – and hence unbridgeable. This is why it partakes only of that abstract – definitively abstract – form known as communication.

Within the space of communication, words, gestures, looks are in a continual state of contiguity, yet they never touch. The fact is that distance and proximity here are simply not relationships obtaining between the body and its surroundings. The screen of our images, the interactive screen, the telecomputing screen, are at once too close and too far away: too close to be true (to have the dramatic intensity of a stage) – and too far away to be false (to embody the collusive distance of artifice). They thus create a dimension that is no longer quite human, an excentric dimension corresponding to the depolarization of space and the indistinctness of bodily forms of expression.

There is no better model of the way in which the computer screen and the mental screen of our own brain are interwoven than Moebius's topology, with its peculiar contiguity of near and far, inside and outside, object and subject within the same spiral. It is in accordance with this same model that information and communication are constantly turning round upon themselves in an incestuous circumvolution, a superficial conflation of subject and object, within and without, question and answer, event and image, and so on. The form is inevitably that of a twisted ring reminiscent of the mathematical symbol for infinity.

The same may be said of our relationship with our 'virtual' machines. Telecomputer Man is assigned to an apparatus, just as the apparatus is assigned to him, by virtue of an involution of each into the other, a refraction of each by the other. The machine does what the human wants it to do, but by the same token the human puts into execution only what the machine has been programmed to do. The operator is working with virtuality: only apparently is the aim to obtain information or to communicate; the real purpose is to explore all the possibilities of a program, rather as a gambler seeks to exhaust the permutations in a game of chance. Consider the way the camera is used now. Its possibilities are no longer those of a subject who 'reflects' the world according to his personal vision; rather, they are the possibilities of the lens, as exploited by the object. The camera is thus a machine that vitiates all will, erases all intentionality and leaves nothing but the pure reflex needed to take pictures. Looking itself disappears without trace, replaced by a lens now in collusion with the object – and hence with an inversion of vision. The magic lies precisely in the subject's retroversion to a camera obscura – the reduction of his vision to the impersonal vision of a mechanical device. In a mirror, it is the subject who gives free rein to the realm of the imaginary. In the camera lens, and on-screen in general, it is the object, potentially, that unburdens itself – to the benefit of all media and telecommunications techniques.

This is why images of *anything* are now a possibility. This is why everything is translatable into computer terms, commutable into digital form, just as each individual is commutable into his own particular genetic code. (The whole object, in fact, is to exhaust all the virtualities of such analogues of the genetic code: this is one of artificial intelligence's most fundamental aspects.) What this means on a more concrete level is that there is no longer any such thing as an act or event which is not refracted into a technical image or onto a screen, any such thing as an action which does not in some sense *want* to be photographed, filmed or tape-recorded, does not desire to be stored in memory so as to become reproducible for all eternity. No such thing as an action which does not aspire to self-transcendence into a virtual eternity – not, now, the durable eternity that follows death, but rather the ephemeral eternity of ever-ramifying artificial memory.

The compulsion of the virtual is the compulsion to exist *in potentia* on all screens, to be embedded in all programs, and it acquires a magical force: the Siren call of the black box.

Where is the freedom in all this? Nowhere! There is no choice here, no final decision. All decisions concerning networks, screens, information or communication are serial in character, partial, fragmentary, fractal. A mere succession of partial decisions, a microscopic series of partial sequences and objectives, constitute as much the photographer's way of proceeding as that of Telecomputer Man in general, or even that called for by our own most trivial television viewing. All such behaviour is structured in quantum fashion, composed of haphazard sequences of discrete decisions. The fascination derives from the pull of the black box, the appeal of an uncertainty which puts paid to our freedom.

Am I a man or a machine? This anthropological question no longer has an answer. We are thus in some sense witness to the end of anthropology, now being conjured away by the most recent machines and technologies. The uncertainty here is born of the perfecting of machine networks, just as sexual uncertainty (Am I a man or a woman? What has the difference between the sexes become?) is born of increasingly sophisticated manipulation of the unconscious and of the body, and just as science's uncertainty about the status of its object is born of the sophistication of analysis in the microsciences.

Am I a man or a machine? There is no ambiguity in the traditional relationship between man and machine: the worker is always, in a way, a stranger to the machine he operates, and alienated by it. But at least he retains the precious status of alienated man. The new technologies, with their new machines, new images and interactive screens, do *not* alienate me. Rather, they form an integrated circuit with me. Video screens, televisions, computers and Minitels resemble nothing so much as contact lenses in that they are so many transparent prostheses, integrated into the body to the point of being almost part of its genetic make-up: they are like pacemakers – or like Philip K. Dick's 'papula', a tiny implant, grafted onto the body at birth as a 'free gift', which serves the organism as an alarm signal. All our relationships with networks and screens, whether willed or not, are of this order. Their structure is one of subordination, not of alienation – the structure of the integrated circuit. Man or machine? Impossible to tell.

Surely the extraordinary success of artificial intelligence is attributable to the fact that it frees us from real intelligence, that by hypertrophying thought as an operational process it frees us from thought's ambiguity and from the insoluble puzzle of its relationship to the world. Surely the success of all these technologies is a result of the way in which they make it impossible even to raise the timeless question of liberty. What a relief! Thanks to the machinery of the virtual, all your problems are over! You are no longer either subject or object, no longer either free or alienated – and no longer either one or the other: you are *the same*, and enraptured by the commutations of that sameness. We have left the hell of other people for the ecstasy of the same, the purgatory of otherness for the artificial paradises of identity. Some might call this an even worse servitude, but Telecomputer Man, having no will of his own, knows nothing of serfdom. Alienation of man by man is a thing of the past: now man is plunged into homeostasis by machines.

PROPHYLAXIS AND VIRULENCE

The growing cerebrality of machines must logically be expected to occasion a technological purification of bodies. Inasmuch as bodies are less and less able to count on their own antibodies, they are more and more in need of protection from outside. An artificial sterilization of all environments must compensate for faltering internal immunological defences. And if these are indeed faltering, it is because the irreversible process often referred to as progress tends to strip the human body and mind of their systems of initiative and defence, reassigning these functions to technical artifacts. Once dispossessed of their defences, human beings become eminently vulnerable to science and technology; dispossessed of their passions, they likewise become eminently vulnerable to psychology and its attendant therapies; similarly, too, once relieved of emotions and illnesses, they become eminently vulnerable to medicine.

Consider the 'Boy in the Bubble', surrounded, in his NASA-donated tent, by an atmospheric distillate of medical knowledge, protected from any conceivable infection by an artificial immune system, 'cuddled' by his mother through the glass, laughing and growing up in an extraterrestrial ambiance under the vigilant eye of science. Here we have the experimental version of the wolf-child, the 'wild child' raised by wolves. The parenting in this case, however, is done by computers.

The Boy in the Bubble is a prefiguration of the future – of that total asepsis, that total extirpation of germs, which is the biological form of transparency. He epitomizes the kind of vacuum-sealed existence hitherto reserved for bacteria and particles in laboratories but now destined for us as, more and more, we are vacuum-pressed like records, vacuum-packed like deep-frozen foods and vacuum-enclosed for death as victims of fanatical therapeutic measures. That we think and reflect in a vacuum is demonstrated by the ubiquitousness of artificial intelligence.

It is not absurd to suppose that the extermination of man begins with the extermination of man's germs. One has only to consider the human being himself, complete with his emotions, his passions, his laughter, his sex and his secretions, to conclude that man is nothing but a dirty little germ – an irrational virus marring a universe of transparency. Once he has been purged, once everything has been cleaned up and all infection – whether of a social or a bacillary kind – has been driven out, then only the virus of sadness will remain in a mortally clean and mortally sophisticated world.

Thought, itself a sort of network of antibodies and natural immune defences, is also highly vulnerable. It is in acute danger of being conveniently replaced by an electronic cerebrospinal bubble from which any animal or metaphysical reflex has been expunged. Even without all the technological advantages of the Boy in the Bubble, we are already living in the bubble ourselves – already, like those characters in Bosch paintings, enclosed in a crystal sphere: a transparent envelope in which we have taken refuge and where we remain, bereft of everything yet overprotected, doomed to artificial immunity, continual transfusions and, at the slightest contact with the world outside, instant death.

This is why we are all losing our defences – why we are all potentially immunodeficient.

All integrated and hyperintegrated systems – the technological system, the social system, even thought itself in artificial intelligence and its derivatives – tend towards the extreme constituted by immunodeficiency. Seeking to eliminate all external aggression, they secrete their own internal virulence, their own malignant reversibility. When a certain saturation point is reached, such systems effect this reversal and undergo this alteration willy-nilly – and thus tend to self-destruct. Their very transparency becomes a threat to them, and the crystal has its revenge.

In a hyperprotected space the body loses all its defences. So sterile are operating rooms that no germ or bacterium can survive there. Yet this is the very place where mysterious, anomalous viral diseases make their appearance. The fact is that viruses proliferate as soon as they find a free space. A world purged of the old forms of infection, a world 'ideal' from the clinical point of view, offers a perfect field of operations for the impalpable and implacable pathology which arises from the sterilization itself.

This is a third-level pathology. Just as our societies are confronting a new kind of violence, born of the paradoxical fact that they are simultaneously both permissive and pacified, so too we face new illnesses, those illnesses which beset bodies overprotected by their artificial, medical or computer-generated shield. This pathology is produced not by accident, nor by anomie, but rather by *anomaly*. The very same thing happens with the social body, where the same causes bring about the same perverse effects, the same unforeseeable dysfunctions – a situation comparable to the genetic disorder that occurs at the cellular level, again occasioned by overprotection, overcoding, overmanagement. The social system, just like the biological body, loses its natural defences in precise proportion to the growing sophistication of its prostheses. Moreover, this unprecedented pathology is unlikely to be effectively conjured away by medicine, because medicine is itself part of the system of overprotection, and contributes to the fanatical protective and preventive measures lavished upon the body. Just as there seems to be no political solution to the problem of terrorism, so there seems to be no biological solution at present to the problems of AIDS and cancer. Indeed, the causes are identical: anomalous symptoms generated at the most fundamental level by the system itself represent a reactive virulence designed to counter, in the first case, a political overmanagement of the social body, and in the second case, a biological overmanagement of the body *tout court*.

At an early stage the evil genie of otherness takes the forms of accident, breakdown, failure. Only later does the viral, epidemic form make its appearance: a virulence that ravages the entire system, and against which the system is defenceless precisely because its very integrity paradoxically engenders this alteration.

Virulence takes hold of a body, a network or other system when that system rejects all its negative components and resolves itself into a combinatorial system of simple elements. It is because a circuit or a network has thus become a *virtual* being, a non-body, that viruses can run riot within it; hence too the much greater vulnerability of 'immaterial' machines as compared with traditional mechanical devices. Virtual and viral go hand in hand. It is because the body itself has become a non-body, a virtual machine, that viruses are taking it over.

It is logical that AIDS (and cancer) should have become the prototypes of our modern pathology, as of all lethal viral onslaughts. Saddling the body with replacement parts and abandoning it to genetic whims inevitably dislocates its systems of defence. A fractal body whose external functions are fated to multiply is, by the same token, fated to suffer internal proliferation at the cellular level. Metastasis occurs – and internal and biological metastases are paralleled by the external metastases constituted by prostheses, networks and ramiform systems.

Under the reign of the virus you are destroyed by your own antibodies. This is the leukaemia of an organism devouring its own defences, precisely because all threat, all adversity, has disappeared. Total prophylaxis is lethal. This is what medicine has failed to grasp: it treats cancer or AIDS as if they were conventional illnesses, when in fact they are illnesses generated by the very success of prophylaxis and medicine, illnesses bred of the disappearance of illnesses, of the elimination of pathogenic forms. We are confronted by a third-level pathology, one that is inaccessible to the pharmacopoeia of an earlier period (characterized by visible causes and mechanically produced effects). Suddenly all afflictions seem to originate in immunodeficiency – rather as all violence now seems to have its roots in terrorism. The onslaught of viruses and their strategies have in a sense taken over the work of the unconscious.

Just as human beings, conceived of as digital machines, have become the preferred field of operations of viral illnesses, so have software networks become the preferred field of operations of electronic viruses. Here too there is no effective prevention or cure: metastasis affects entire networks, and desymbolized machine languages offer no more resistance to viral infection than do desymbolized bodies. The familiar breakdowns and mechanical accidents of earlier times responded to good old-fashioned reparative medicine, but for these sudden weakenings, sudden anomalies, sudden 'stabs in the back' by antibodies, we have no remedy. We knew how to cure illnesses of forms; against pathologies of formulas we are without defences. Having everywhere sacrificed the natural balance of forms in favour of an artificial concordance between code and formula, we have unleashed the threat of a far graver disorder, of a destabilization without precedent. Having turned the body and language into artificial systems in thrall to artificial intelligence, we have abandoned them not only to artificial stupidity but also to all the viral aberrations generated by this irreversible artificiality.

Viral attack is the pathology of the closed circuit, of the integrated circuit, of promiscuity and of the chain reaction – in a broad and metaphorical sense, a pathology of incest. He who lives by the same shall die by the same. The absence of otherness secretes another, intangible otherness: the absolute other of the virus.

That AIDS should have struck homosexuals and drug-users first is a reflection of the incestuousness of groups which function as closed circuits. We had known for a long time that haemophilia was linked to consanguine marriages and predominantly endogamous social systems. Even the strange sickness that affected cypress trees for so long turned out to be a sort of virus attributable to a lessening of the temperature difference between winter and summer – to a promiscuity, so to speak, of the seasons. The spectre of the Same had struck again. In every compulsion to resemblance, every extradition of difference, in all contiguity of things and their own image, all conflation of beings and their own code, lies the threat of an incestuous virulence, a diabolical otherness boding the breakdown of all this humming machinery. This is the reappearance of the principle of Evil in a new guise. No morality or guilt is implied, however: the principle of Evil is simply synonymous with the principle of reversal, with the turns of fate. In systems undergoing total positivization – and hence desymbolization – evil is equivalent, in all its forms, to the fundamental rule of reversibility.

Still, there is an ambiguity in this very virulence. AIDS serves to justify a new prohibition on sex – no longer a moral prohibition but a functional one, one directed not at sex *per se* but merely at its unhindered circulation. The current is to be interrupted, the flow stopped. But this runs counter to all the commandments of modernity, according to which sex, money and information must circulate freely. Everything is supposed to be fluid, everything should accelerate inexorably. The placing of strictures upon sexuality on grounds of viral risk seems as absurd as halting foreign-exchange dealings because they foster speculation or wild fluctuations in the value of the dollar. Unthinkable! And yet, all of a sudden, there it is: no more sex. Is there a contradiction in the system here?

Could it be that this suspension has a paradoxical aim, one bound up with the equally paradoxical aim of sexual liberation? We are acquainted with that spontaneous self-regulation of systems whereby they themselves produce accidents or slowdowns in order to survive. No society can live without in a sense opposing its own value system: it has to have such a system, yet it must at the same time define itself in contradistinction to it. At present we live according to at least two principles: that of sexual liberation and that of communication and information. And everything suggests that the species itself, via the threat of AIDS, is generating an antidote to its principle of sexual liberation; that by means of cancer, which is a breakdown of the genetic code, it is setting up a resistance to the all-powerful principle of cybernetic control; and that the viral onslaught in general signals its sabotaging of the universal principle of communication.

What if all this betokened a refusal of the obligatory flows of sperm, sex and words, a refusal of forced communication, programmed information and sexual promiscuity? What if it heralded a vital resistance to the spread of flows, circuits and networks – at the cost, it is true, of a new and lethal pathology, but one, nevertheless, that would protect us from something even worse? If so, then AIDS and cancer would be the price we are paying for our own system: an attempt to cure its *banal* virulence by recourse to a *fatal* form. Nobody can predict the effectiveness of such an exorcism, but the question has to be asked: What is cancer a resistance to, what even worse eventuality is it saving us from? (Could it be the total hegemony of genetic coding?) What is AIDS a resistance to, what even worse eventuality is it saving us from? (Could it be a sexual epidemic, a sort of total promiscuity?) The same goes for drugs: all melodramatics aside, what exactly do they protect us from, from what even worse scourge do they offer us an avenue of escape? (Could it be the brutalizing effects of rationality, normative socialization and universal conditioning?) As for terrorism, does not its secondary, reactive violence shield us from an epidemic of consensus, from an ever-increasing political leukaemia and degeneration and from the imperceptible transparency of the State? All things are ambiguous and reversible. After all, it is neurosis that offers human beings their most effective protection against madness. AIDS may thus be seen not as a divine punishment, but as quite the opposite – as a defensive abreaction on the part of the species against the danger of a total promiscuity, a total loss of identity through the proliferation and speed-up of networks.

The high degree to which AIDS, terrorism, crack cocaine or computer viruses mobilize the popular imagination should tell us that they are more than anecdotal occurrences in an irrational world. The fact is that they contain within them the whole logic of our system: these events are merely the spectacular expression of that system. They all hew to the same agenda of virulence and radiation, an agenda whose very power over the imagination is of a viral character: a single terrorist act obliges a reconsideration of politics as a whole in the light of terrorism's claims; an outbreak of AIDS, even a statistically insignificant one, forces us to view the whole spectrum of disease in the light of the immunodeficiency thesis; and the mildest of computer viruses, whether it vitiates the Pentagon's memory banks or merely erases a shower of on-line Christmas messages, has the potential to destabilize all data contained in information systems.

Whence the special status of such extreme phenomena – and of catastrophe in general, understood as an anomalous turn of events. The secret order of catastrophe resides in the affinity between all these processes, as in their homology with the system as a whole. Order within disorder: all extreme phenomena are consistent both with respect to each other and with respect to the whole that they constitute. This means that it is useless to appeal to some supposed rationality of the system against that system's outgrowths. The vanity of seeking to abolish these extreme phenomena is absolute. Moreover, they are destined to become more extreme still as our systems grow more sophisticated. And this is in fact a good thing – for they are the leading edge of therapy here. In these transparent, homeostatic or homeofluid systems there is no longer any such thing as a strategy of Good against Evil, there is only the pitting of Evil against Evil – a strategy of last resort. Indeed, we really have no choice in the matter: we simply watch as the lesser evil – homeopathic virulence – deploys its forces. AIDS, crack and computer viruses are merely outcroppings of the catastrophe; nine-tenths of it remain buried in the virtual. The full-blown, the absolute catastrophe would be a true omnipresence of all networks, a total transparency of all data – something from which, for now, computer viruses preserve us. Thanks to them, we shall not be going straight to the culminating point of the development of information and communications, which is to say: death. These viruses are both the first sign of this lethal transparency and its alarm signal. One is put in mind of a fluid travelling at increasing speed, forming eddies and anomalous countercurrents which arrest or dissipate its flow. Chaos imposes a limit upon what would otherwise hurtle into an absolute void. The secret disorder of extreme phenomena, then, plays a prophylactic role by opposing its chaos to any escalation of order and transparency to their extremes. But these phenomena notwithstanding, we are already witness to the beginning of the end of a certain way of thinking. Similarly, in the case of sexual liberation, we are already witness to the beginning of the end of a certain type of gratification. If total sexual promiscuity were ever achieved, however, sex itself would self-destruct in the resulting asexual flood. Much the same may be said of economic exchange. Financial speculation, as turbulence, makes the boundless extension of real transactions impossible. By precipitating an instantaneous circulation of value – by, as it were, electrocuting the economic model – it also short-circuits the catastrophe of a free and universal commutability – such a total liberation being the true catastrophic tendency of value.

In the face of the threats of a total weightlessness, an unbearable lightness of being, a universal promiscuity and a linearity of processes liable to plunge us into the void, the sudden whirlpools that we dub catastrophes are really the thing that saves us from catastrophe. Anomalies and aberrations of this kind re-create zones of gravity and density that counter dispersion. It may be hazarded that this is how our societies secrete their own peculiar version of an accursed share, much after the fashion of those tribal peoples who used to dispose of their surplus population by means of an oceanic suicide: the homeopathic suicide of a few serving to maintain the homeostatic balance of the group.

So the actual catastrophe may turn out to be a carefully modulated strategy of our species – or, more precisely, our viruses, our extreme phenomena, which are most definitively real, albeit localized, may be what allow us to preserve the energy of that *virtual* catastrophe which is the motor of all our processes, whether economic or political, artistic or historical.

To epidemic, contagion, chain reactions and proliferation we owe at once the worst and the best. The worst is metastasis in cancer, fanaticism in politics, virulence in the biological sphere and rumour in the sphere of information. Fundamentally, though, all these also partake of the best, for the process of chain reaction is an immoral process, beyond good and evil, and hence reversible. It must be said, moreover, that we greet both worst and best with the same fascination.

That it should be possible for certain processes – economic, political, linguistic, cultural, sexual, even theoretical and scientific – to set aside the limitations of meaning and proceed by immediate contagion, according to the laws of the pure reciprocal immanencies of things among themselves rather than the laws of their transcendence or their referentiality – that this is possible poses an enigma to reason while offering a marvellous alternative to the imagination.

One has but to consider the phenomenon of fashion, which has never been satisfactorily explained. Fashion is the despair of sociology and aesthetics: a prodigious contagion of forms in which chain reactions struggle for supremacy over the logic of distinctions. The pleasure of fashion is undeniably cultural in origin, but does it not stem even more clearly from a flaring, unmediated consensus generated by the interplay of signs? Moreover, fashions fade away like epidemics once they have ravaged the imagination, once the virus has run its course. The price to be paid in terms of waste is always exorbitant, yet everyone consents. The marvellous in our societies resides in this ultra-rapid circulation of signs at a surface level (as opposed to the ultra-slow circulation of meanings). We love being contaminated by this process, and not having to think about it. This is a viral onslaught as noxious as the plague, yet no moral sociology, no philosophical reason, will ever extirpate it. Fashion is an irreducible phenomenon because it partakes of a crazy, viral, mediationless form of communication which operates so fast for the sole reason that it never passes via the mediation of meaning.

Anything that bypasses mediation is a source of pleasure. In seduction there is a movement from the one to the other which does not pass via the same. (In cloning, it is the opposite: the movement is from the same to the same without passage via the other; and cloning holds great fascination for us.) In metamorphosis, the shift is from one form to another without passing via meaning. In poetry, from one sign to another without passing via the reference. The collapsing of distances, of intervening spaces, always produces a kind of intoxication. What does speed itself mean to us if not the fact of going from one place to another without traversing time, from one moment to another without passing via duration and movement? Speed is marvellous: time alone is wearisome.

DRIVES AND REPULSIONS

The homogenization of circuits in an ideal universe of synthesis and prosthesis, a universe which is positive, consensual and synchronous – all this
makes for a world that is unacceptable. Not only does the body rebel against
grafts or artificial replacement parts, but the mind too rises up against the
synergy imposed upon it by producing countless forms of *allergy*. Abreaction,
rejection and allergy are manifestations of a singular kind of energy, a visceral
energy which has replaced negativity and critical revolt and bred our time's
most emblematic phenomena: viral pathologies, terrorism, drugs, delinquency
– even such reputedly positive features as the cult of performance and a mass
production hysteria, which have much more to do with the compulsion to get
rid of something than with the drive to create anything at all. Today we are
driven far less by drives proper than by considerations of expulsion and
repulsion. Natural disasters themselves suggest a kind of allergy – a rejection
by nature of the operational dominance of human agency. As negativity
agonizes, such events constitute an irreducible sign of violence, a precious and

supernatural sign of denial. Moreover, their virulence, by its contagiousness, frequently precipitates social disorder.

The great drives or impulses, with their positive, elective and attractive powers, are gone. We desire still, but in the feeblest way only; our tastes are less and less highly determined. The constellations of taste and of desire, like that of the will, have been blown apart – by what mechanism, we do not know. By contrast, the constellations of unwillingness, of repulsion and disgust, are more solid than ever. It seems that this has generated a new energy, a counter-energy, a force that has taken the place of desire in us, a viral abreaction in response to whatever has replaced the world, the body and sex for us. Today only distaste is determined – tastes are determinate no longer. Only rejections are violent – projects are violent no longer. Our actions, our undertakings, our sicknesses have less and less in the way of 'objective' motives: they arise for the most part from a concealed self-disgust, an unacknowledged empty legacy which causes us to try to get rid of our energy by whatever means. A kind of exorcism, then, rather than a will to action. Could this be the principle of Evil in a new form, one not far removed from magic – whose epicentre, as we know, is, precisely, exorcism?

In Simmel's words, 'Negation is the simplest thing imaginable. That is why the broad masses, whose component elements cannot achieve agreement as to goals, come together here.' It is useless to expect a positive opinion or a critical will from the masses, for they have none: all they have is an undifferentiated power, the power to *reject*. Their strength flows solely from what they are able to expel, to negate – and that is, first and foremost, any project that goes beyond them, any class or understanding that transcends them. There is something here of a philosophy of cunning born of the most brutal experience – the experience of animals, or of peasants: 'They won't put that over on us again, we won't fall for their calls to sacrifice, or listen to their pie in the sky.' Profound disgust for the political order – though one that may well coexist with specific political opinions. Disgust for the pretension and transcendence of power, for the inevitability and abomination of the political sphere. Where once there were political passions, we now find only the violence peculiar to a fundamental disgust with everything political.

Power itself is founded largely on disgust. The whole of advertising, the whole of political discourse, is a public insult to the intelligence, to reason – but an insult in which we collaborate, abjectly subscribing to a silent interaction. The day of hidden persuasion is over: those who govern us now resort unapologetically to arm-twisting pure and simple. The prototype here was a banker got up like a vampire, saying, 'I am after you for your money'. A decade has already gone by since this kind of obscenity was introduced, with the government's blessing, into our social mores. At the time we thought the ad feeble because of its aggressive vulgarity. In point of fact it was a prophetic commercial, full of intimations of the future shape of social relationships, because it operated, precisely, in terms of disgust, avidity and rape. The same goes for pornographic and food advertising, which are also powered by shamelessness and lust, by a strategic logic of violation and anxiety. Nowadays you can seduce a woman with the words, 'I am interested in your cunt'. The same kind of crassness has triumphed in the realm of art, whose mounds of trivia may be reduced to a single pronouncement of the type, 'What we want from you is stupidity and bad taste'. And the fact is that we do succumb to this mass extortion, with its subtle infusion of guilt.

It is true in a sense that nothing really disgusts us any more. In our eclectic culture, which embraces the debris of all others in a promiscuous confusion, nothing is unacceptable. But for this very reason disgust is nevertheless on the increase – the desire to spew out this promiscuity, this indifference to everything no matter how bad, this viscous adherence of opposites. To the extent that this happens, what is on the increase is disgust over the lack of disgust. An allergic temptation to reject everything *en bloc*: to refuse all the gentle brain-washing, the soft-sold overfeeding, the tolerance, the pressure to embrace synergy and consensus.

All the talk of immunity, antibodies, grafting and rejection should not surprise anyone. In periods of scarcity, absorption and assimilation are the order of the day. In periods of abundance, rejection and expulsion are the chief concerns. Today, generalized communication and surplus information threaten to overwhelm all human defences. Symbolic space, the mental space of judgement, has no protection whatsoever. Not only am I unable to decide whether something is beautiful or not, original or not, but the biological organism itself is at a loss to know what is good for it and what is not. In such circumstances everything becomes a bad object, and the only primitive defence is abreaction or rejection.

Laughter itself is more often than not a vital abreaction to the disgust we feel for the monstrous mixing and promiscuity that confront us. But for all that we may gag on the absence of differentiation, it still fascinates us. We love to mix everything up, even if it simultaneously repels us. The reaction whereby the organism seeks to preserve its symbolic integrity is a vital one, even if the price paid is life itself (as in the rejection of a transplanted heart). Why would bodies *not* resist the arbitrary swapping of organs and cells? Also: why do cells, in cancer, refuse to carry out their assigned functions?

THE MIRROR OF
TERRORISM

And why does terrorism exist, if not as a violent form of abreaction in the social realm?

The most striking thing about events such as those that took place at the Heysel Stadium, Brussels, in 1985, is not their violence *per se* but the way in which this violence was given worldwide currency by television, and in the process turned into a travesty of itself.

'How is such barbarity possible in the late twentieth century?' This is a false question. There is no atavistic resurgence of some archaic type of violence. The violence of old was both more enthusiastic and more sacrificial than ours. Today's violence, the violence produced by our hypermodernity, is terror. A simulacrum of violence, emerging less from passion than from the screen: a violence in the nature of the image. Violence exists potentially in the emptiness of the screen, in the hole the screen opens in the mental universe. So true is this that it is advisable not to be in a public place where television is operating, considering the high probability that its very presence will precipitate a violent event. The media are always on the scene in advance of terrorist violence. This is what makes terrorism a peculiarly modern form – far more modern than the 'objective' causes to which we seek to attribute it: political, sociological or psychological approaches are simply not capable of accounting for such events.

Another remarkable aspect of a happening like this is that it is in some way expected. We all collude in the anticipation of a fatal outcome, even if we are emotionally affected or shaken when it occurs. The Brussels police have been criticized for failing to avert the explosion of violence at the Heysel Stadium, but what no police could ever guard against is the sort of fascination, of mass appeal, exercised by the terrorist model.

Occurrences of this kind represent a sudden crystallization of latent violence. They are not confrontations between hostile forces, not a clash between antagonistic passions, but the product of listless and indifferent forces (among them television's inert audience). The violence of football hooligans is an aggravated form of indifference, one which has such resonance only because it is based on a lethal crystallization of this kind. Fundamentally, such violence is not so much an event as the explosive form assumed by an absence of events. Or rather, the *implosive* form: and what implodes here is the political void (rather than the resentment of some particular group), the silence of history which has been repressed at the level of individual psychology, and the indifference and silence of everyone. We are dealing, therefore, not with irrational episodes in the life of our society, but instead with something that is completely in accord with that society's accelerating plunge into the void.

There is another logic at work here, too, the logic of attempted role reversal: spectators (English fans, in this case) turn themselves into actors; usurping the role of the protagonists (players), under the gaze of the media, they invent their own spectacle (which – we may as well admit it – is somewhat more fascinating than the official one). Now is this not precisely what is expected of the modern spectator? Is he not supposed to abandon his spectatorish inertia and intervene in the spectacle himself? Surely this is the leitmotiv

76

of the entire culture of participation? Curiously, it is in events of this kind that modern hypersociality of the participatory variety is actualized – its own best efforts notwithstanding. Deplore it as one might, the fact is that two hundred seats smashed up at a rock concert is a sign of success. Where exactly does participation pass over into *too much* participation? The answer to this question – never acknowledged in the discourse of participation – is that 'good' participation ends where *signs* of participation begin. Of course, things do not always work out that way.

The Romans were straightforward enough to mount spectacles of this kind, complete with wild beasts and gladiators, in the full light of day. We can put on such shows only in the wings, as it were – accidentally, or illegally, all the while denouncing them on moral grounds. (Not that this prevents us from disseminating them worldwide as fodder for TV audiences: the few minutes of film from the Heysel Stadium were the most often broadcast images of the year.) Even the 1984 Olympic Games in Los Angeles were transformed into a giant parade, a worldwide show which, just like the Berlin Games of 1936, took place in an atmosphere of terrorism created by power's need to show off its muscles: the worldwide spectacle of sport was thus turned into a Cold War strategy – an utter corruption of the Olympic ideal. Once wrenched away from its basic principle, sport can be pressed into the service of any end whatsoever: as a parade of prestige or of violence, it slips (to use Roger Caillois's terminology) from play founded on competition and representation to circus-like play, play based on the pull of vertigo.

Nor is politics immune from this trend. Behind the tragedy at the Heysel Stadium, in fact, lies a kind of state terrorism. This is not manifested solely in carefully programmed actions (the CIA, Israel, Iran, etc.). For there is also a wilful pursuit of draconian policies, policies of provocation with regard to a country's own citizens, attempts to fill entire sectors of the population with despair, to drive them to the brink of suicide: all of this is part and parcel of the policies of a number of modern states. Mrs Thatcher successfully destroyed the miners by means of just such a calculated bloody-mindedness: the strikers ended up discrediting themselves in the eyes of society. She has a similar strategy towards unemployed hooligans: it is as though she turns them into commandos herself, then sends them abroad; she condemns them, of course, but their brutality remains the very same brutality that she demonstrates in the exercise of her power. Liquidation policies of this kind, more or less drastic in their application, are the stock in trade, justified by the appeal to crisis, of all modern states. They inevitably entail extreme measures of the sort mentioned, which are merely the diverted effects of a terrorism *to which the State is in no way opposed*.

As soon as it becomes impossible for states to attack and destroy one another, they turn almost automatically against their own peoples, their own territories; a sort of civil war or internecine conflict begins between the State and its natural referent. Is it not in fact the fate of every sign, every signifying and representative agency, to abolish its natural referent?

Certainly this is the inevitable outcome in the political realm, a fact of which both represented and representatives are perfectly – albeit obscurely – aware. We are all Machiavellians without knowing it, by virtue of our obscure consciousness of the fact that representation is no more than a dialectical fiction concealing a duel to the death between the two parties involved, and that it mobilizes a will to power and a will to destroy the other which may end up with the destruction of the self through voluntary servitude: all power is composed of the Hegemony of the Prince and the Holocaust of the People.

Neither a represented people nor a legitimate sovereign is now the issue. That political configuration has given way to a contest in which there is no longer any question of a social contract: a transpolitical contest between an agency orientated towards totalitarian self-reference on the one hand, and sardonic or refractory, agnostic and infantile masses on the other (masses which no longer speak, though they chat). This is the hypochondriacal condition of the body devouring its own organs. Powers – States – have set about destroying their own cities, their own landscapes, their own substance and, indeed, themselves with a fury that can be compared only to the fury they once directed towards the destruction of their enemies.

In the absence of an original political strategy (which is indeed perhaps no longer possible), and in view of the impossibility of a rational management of the social realm, the State becomes desocialized. It no longer works on the basis of political will, but instead on the basis of intimidation, dissuasion, simulation, provocation or spectacular solicitation. It invents a politics of disaffection and indifference. This is the *transpolitical reality* behind all official policies: a cynical bias towards the elimination of the social. Soccer hooligans are merely the most extreme manifestation of this transpolitical conjuncture: they carry participation to its tragic limit, while at the same time daring the State to respond with violence, to liquidate them. In this respect they are no different from terrorists. The reason why such tactics fascinate us, quite apart from moral considerations, is that they constitute a paroxystically up-to-the-minute model, a mirror-image of our own disappearance *qua* political society – a disappearance that 'political' pseudo-events strive so desperately to camouflage.

Another recent episode forms a pendant to the events of the Heysel Stadium: in September 1987, in Madrid, a Real Madrid–Naples European Cup match took place at night in a completely empty stadium, without a single spectator, as a consequence of disciplinary action taken by the International Federation in response to the excesses of the Madrid supporters at an earlier game. Thousands of fans besieged the stadium, but no one got in. The match was relayed in its entirety via television.

A ban of this kind could never do away with the chauvinistic passions surrounding soccer, but it does perfectly exemplify the terroristic hyperrealism of our world, a world where a 'real' event occurs in a vacuum, stripped of its context and visible only from afar, televisually. Here we have a sort of surgically accurate prefiguration of the events of our future: events so minimal that they might well not need take place at all – along with their maximal enlargement on screens. No one will have directly experienced the actual course of such happenings, but everyone will have received an image of them. A pure event, in other words, devoid of any reference in nature, and readily susceptible to replacement by synthetic images.

This phantom football match should obviously be seen in conjunction with the Heysel Stadium game, when the real event, football, was once again eclipsed – on this occasion by a much more dramatic form of violence. There is always the danger that this kind of transition may occur, that spectators may cease to be spectators and slip into the role of victims or murderers, that sport may cease to be sport and be transformed into terrorism: that is why the public must simply be eliminated, to ensure that the only event occurring is strictly televisual in nature. Every real referent must disappear so that the event may become acceptable on television's mental screen.

Political events themselves likewise unfold, in a sense, in an empty stadium (the empty form of representation) whence any real public has been expelled because of potentially too lively passions, and whence nothing emerges now save a television retranscription (CRT images, statistics, poll results . . .). Politics still works, even captivates us, but subtly everything begins to operate as though some International Political Federation had suspended the public for an indeterminate period and expelled it from all stadiums to ensure the objective conduct of the match. Such is our present transpolitical arena: a transparent form of public space from which all the actors have been withdrawn – and a pure form of the event from which all passion has been removed.

WHATEVER HAPPENED TO EVIL?

Terrorism in all its forms is the transpolitical mirror of evil. For the real problem, the only problem, is: where did Evil go? And the answer is: everywhere – because the anamorphosis of modern forms of Evil knows no bounds. In a society which seeks – by prophylactic measures, by annihilating its own natural referents, by whitewashing violence, by exterminating all germs and all of the accursed share, by performing cosmetic surgery on the negative – to concern itself solely with quantified management and with the discourse of the Good, in a society where it is no longer possible to speak Evil, Evil has metamorphosed into all the viral and terroristic forms that obsess us.

The force of anathema and the power of speaking Evil are no longer ours. But they have resurfaced elsewhere – witness Ayatollah Khomeini in the matter of Salman Rushdie. Quite apart from performing a *tour de force* whereby the West has been obliged to hold this particular hostage itself, whereby Rushdie has in a way been obliged to hold himself entirely hostage, the Ayatollah has offered spectacular proof of how it is possible to overturn all existing power relations through the symbolic force of an utterance.

Confronting the entire world, his tally utterly negative in the distribution of political, military and economic forces, the Ayatollah had but one weapon at his disposal, yet that weapon, though it had no material reality, came close to being the absolute weapon: the principle of Evil. The negation of all Western values – of progress, rationality, political ethics, democracy, and so on. By rejecting the universal consensus on all these Good Things, Khomeini became the recipient of the energy of Evil, the Satanic energy of the rejected, the glamour of the accursed share. He alone now holds the tribune because he alone has upheld against all comers the Machiavellian principle of Evil, because he alone is ready to speak Evil and exorcize Evil, because he alone allows himself to incarnate that principle on the basis of terror. His motivations are unintelligible to us. On the other hand, we cannot fail to recognize the superiority that his posture assures him over a West where the possibility of evoking Evil does not exist and every last trace of negativity is smothered by the virtual consensus that prevails. Our political authorities themselves are but mere shadows of their declared functions. For power exists solely by virtue of its symbolic ability to designate the Other, the Enemy, what is at stake, what threatens us, what is Evil. Today this ability has been lost, and, correspondingly, there exists no opposition able or willing to designate power as Evil. We have become very weak in terms of Satanic, ironic, polemical and antagonistic energy; our societies have become fanatically soft – or softly fanatical. By hunting down all of the accursed share in ourselves and allowing only positive values free rein, we have made ourselves dramatically vulnerable to even the mildest of viral attacks, including that of the Ayatollah – who, for one, is not suffering from immunodeficiency. What is more, we end up treating Khomeini, in the name of the rights of man, as 'Absolute Evil' (Mitterrand) – in other words, we respond to his imprecation in its own terms, something which runs counter to the rules of any enlightened discourse. (Do we now ever describe a mad person as 'mad'? As a matter of fact, we are so terrified of Evil, so greedy for euphemisms to denote the Other, misfortune, or other irreducibles, that we no longer even refer to a cripple as such.) Little wonder, then, that someone capable of speaking the language of Evil literally, even triumphantly, should have precipitated such an attack of weak knees among Western cultures (all the petitions of the intellectuals notwithstanding). The fact is that legality, good conscience and even reason itself end up collaborating with the curse. They have no choice but to call down all the resources of anathema, but by that very fact they fall into the trap of the principle of Evil, which is contagious in its essence. So who won? The Ayatollah, unquestionably. Of course we still have the power to destroy him, but on the symbolic level he is the victor, and symbolic power is always superior to the power of arms and money. This is, in a way, the revenge of the Other World. The Third World has never been able to throw down a real challenge to the West. As for the USSR, which for several decades incarnated Evil for the West, it is obviously in the process of quietly lining up on the side of Good, on the side of an extremely moderate way of managing things. (By a marvellous irony the USSR has even put itself forward as mediator between the West and the Satan of Teheran, having defended Western values for five years in Afghanistan without anyone quite realizing it.)

The reactions of fascination, attraction and worldwide repulsion unleashed by the Rushdie death sentence are reminiscent of the depressurization of an aircraft cabin that occurs when the plane's fuselage is breached or cracked. (Even when such an event is accidental, it resembles a terrorist act.) Everything is sucked violently out into the void as a result of the variation in pressure between inside and out. All that is needed is for a small rift or hole to be made in the ultra-thin envelope that separates two worlds. Terrorism, the taking of hostages, is *par excellence* an act that punches just such a hole in a universe (ours) that is both artificial and artificially protected. Islam as a whole – Islam *as it is*, not the Islam of the Middle Ages: the Islam that has to be evaluated in *strategic* terms, not moral or religious ones – is in the process of creating a vacuum around the Western system (including the countries of Eastern Europe) and from time to time puncturing this system with a single act or utterance, so that all our values are suddenly engulfed by the void. Islam exerts no revolutionary pressure upon the Western universe, nor is there any prospect of its converting or conquering the West: it is content to destabilize it by means of viral attacks of this kind, in the name of a principle of Evil against which we are defenceless and on the basis of the virtual catastrophe constituted by the difference in pressure between the two worlds, on the basis of the perpetual threat to a protected universe (ours), of a brutal depressurization of the atmosphere (the values) that we breathe. The fact is that a good deal of oxygen has already escaped from our Western world through all kinds of fissures and interstices. We would be well advised, therefore, to keep our oxygen masks on.

The Ayatollah's strategy is a remarkably modern one, whatever people might prefer to think. Far more modern than our own, in fact, because it consists in subtly injecting archaic elements into a modern context: a *fatwa*, a death sentence, an imprecation – no matter what. If only our Western universe were solid, all this would be meaningless. In the event, however, our whole system is swallowed up, and serves as a sound box – as a superconductor for the virus. What does this mean? Here again we see the revenge of the Other World: we have visited so many germs and sicknesses, so many epidemics and ideologies, upon the rest of the world, which was utterly defenceless against them, that our present defencelessness against a vile, archaic microorganism seems to be a truly ironic twist of fate.

Even the hostages themselves become a seat of infection. In his recent book *Le Métier d'otage* [Profession: Hostage], Alain Bosquet has shown how the hostage, as a tiny portion of the Western world sucked out into the void, cannot and does not ever want to return home; this is certainly in part attributable to the victim's loss of self-esteem, but it is also because his own people, his own country and his own fellow-citizens are diminished collectively by their forced passivity and their ordinary cowardice – and also by the act of negotiating itself, which is both degrading *per se* and ultimately useless. Beyond the question of negotiation, every hostage-taking bears witness to the unavoidable spinelessness of entire societies with respect to even the most insignificant of their members. This indifference on the part of the community is echoed by each individual's indifference towards that community: this is how we operate in the West – badly – and such is the political impoverishment pitilessly illuminated by the strategy of taking hostages. The destabilization of a single individual effectively destabilizes a whole system. This is why released hostages can never forgive their compatriots for making heroes out of them. (Such 'heroes' are, in any case, immediately hustled out of the public's view.)

We cannot read the Ayatollah's thoughts, nor can we see into the hearts of Muslims. What we can do, however, is reject the feeble notion that everything can be laid at the door of religious fanaticism. I very much fear, however, that we are ill armed to counter the symbolic violence of the Ayatollah's challenge: at this very moment we are striving to expunge the Terror from our memory of the French Revolution, as we prepare to mount a commemoration which, like the consensus, resembles nothing so much as an inflatable structure. How can we ever confront this new violence if we prefer to eradicate even the violence of our own history?

We can no longer speak Evil.

All we can do is discourse on the rights of man – a discourse which is pious, weak, useless and hypocritical, its supposed value deriving from the Enlightenment belief in a natural attraction of the Good, from an idealized view of human relationships (whereas Evil can manifestly be dealt with only by means of Evil).

What is more, even this Good *qua* ideal value is invariably deployed in a self-defensive, austerity-loving, negative and reactive mode. All the talk is of the minimizing of Evil, the prevention of violence: nothing but *security*. This is the condescending and depressive power of good intentions, a power that can dream of nothing except rectitude in the world, that refuses even to consider a bending of Evil, or an intelligence of Evil.

There can be a 'right' to speech only if speech is defined as the 'free' expression of an individual. Where speech is conceived of as a form implying reciprocity, collusion, antagonism or seduction, the notion of right can have no possible meaning.

Is there such a thing as a right to desire, a right to the unconscious, or a right to pleasure? The idea is absurd. This is what makes the sexual liberation movement ridiculous when it talks about rights, and what makes our 'commemoration' of the Revolution ridiculous when the rights of man are evoked.

The 'right to live' is an idea that sets all pious souls atremble, but when this idea evolves into the right to die, the absurdity of the whole business becomes obvious. For, after all, dying (and living too) is a destiny, a fate – be it happy or unhappy – and certainly not a right.

Why not demand the 'right' to be a man or a woman? Or, for that matter, a Leo, an Aquarius or a Cancer? But what would it *mean* to be a man or a woman if it were a right? What makes life exciting is the fact that you have been placed on one side or the other of the sexual divide, and you must take it from there. Those are the rules of the game, and it makes no sense to break them. No one can stop me from claiming the right to move my knight in a straight line on the chessboard, but where does it get me? Rights in such matters are idiotic.

The right to work: yes, we have reached that point, thanks to a savage irony. The right to unemployment! The right to strike! No one can even see the surreal humour of such things any more. Occasionally, though, a certain black humour does burst out here, as when an American condemned to death claims the right to be executed despite the efforts of umpteen human-rights organizations to obtain a stay of execution. This is where things get interesting. The list of rights turns out to include not a few bizarre varieties: the Israelis, for example, claim as a sort of right the fact that there are criminals among their number – whereas from time immemorial, Jews were only victims. Now at last they can enjoy the officially endorsed luxury of criminality!

There can be no doubt either that the USSR, with Chernobyl, the Armenian earthquake and the foundering of a nuclear submarine, has taken a giant step towards an extension of the rights of man (indeed, beyond the accords of Helsinki or elsewhere), for the Soviets have clearly laid claim to the *right to catastrophe*. It is indeed your most fundamental and essential right – your right to accidents, to crime, to error, to Evil, to the worst as well as to the best – which, far more than your right to happiness, makes you a human being worthy of the name.

In the sphere of rights the irresistible trend is towards a situation where, if something can be taken for granted, all rights are otiose, whereas if a right must be demanded, it means that the battle is already lost; thus the very call for rights to water, air and space indicates that all these things are already on the way out. Similarly the evocation of a right to reply signals the absence of any dialogue, and so on.

The rights of the individual lose their meaning as soon as the individual is no longer an alienated being, deprived of his own being, a stranger to himself, as has long been the case in societies of exploitation and scarcity. In his postmodern avatar, however, the individual is a self-referential and self-operating unit. Under such circumstances the human-rights system becomes totally inadequate and illusory: the flexible, mobile individual of variable geometric form is no longer a subject with rights but has become, rather, a tactician and promoter of his own existence whose point of reference is not some agency of law but merely the efficiency of his own functioning or performance.

Yet it is precisely now that the rights of man are acquiring a worldwide resonance. They constitute the only ideology that is currently available – which is as much as to say that human rights are the zero point of ideology, the sole outstanding balance of history. Human rights and ecology are the two teats of the consensus. The current world charter is that of the New Political Ecology.

Ought we to view this apotheosis of human rights as the irresistible rise of stupidity, as a masterpiece which, though imperilled, is liable to light up the coming *fin de siècle* in the full glare of the consensus?

NECROSPECTIVE

The vain quarrel over Heidegger has no philosophical significance of its own; it is merely symptomatic of a weakness of present-day thought, which, being unable to find any new impetus, returns obsessionally to its reference points; and now, as the end of the century approaches, painfully relives its primal scene, which dates from the century's early years. In a more general way the fuss over Heidegger is symptomatic of the collective revival mania that has overtaken our society as the time for passing the last hundred years in review draws near: there is thus a revival of interest in fascism, in Nazism, in the extermination; and here too there is a temptation to reopen the file on the historical primal scene, to whitewash the dead, to put the balance straight. At the same time, however, there is a perverse fascination with returning to the source of the violence: a collective hallucinatory vision of the historical truth of Evil. Our imaginative powers must indeed be in a feeble state at the moment, our indifference towards our own situation and our own thinking must indeed be immense, for us to be resorting to such regressive thaumaturgics.

Heidegger is accused of having been a Nazi. In point of fact it barely matters whether the aim is to indict him or defend him on this charge; both sides fall into the same trap, both sides are guilty of a low form of thought, a thought so debilitated that it no longer has either confidence in its own antecedents or the force to transcend them, while what little vision it retains is squandered in impeachment, complaint, self-justification and historical verification. Scrutinizing the ambiguities of its masters (even toppling them from their pedestals as master-thinkers), philosophy is in a strictly defensive posture; the same goes for our society as a whole, which, having failed to generate a new history, is doomed to chew over the old one in order to prove its own existence – including the existence of its past crimes. But what does such a proof amount to? It is really only because we have disappeared politically and historically today (and therein lies our problem) that we seek to prove that we died between 1940 and 1945, at Auschwitz or in Hiroshima – which at least makes for a *strong* history. We are like the Armenians, who wear themselves out trying to prove that they were massacred in 1917 – a proof that is unattainable, useless, yet in some sense vital. It is because philosophy too has disappeared today (and therein lies *its* problem, for how can something live if it has disappeared?) that it seeks to demonstrate that it was definitively compromised along with Heidegger, or rendered aphasic by Auschwitz. All of this reflects a desperate historical search for a posthumous truth, a posthumous absolution – and it comes at a moment when there is, precisely, insufficient truth available to ensure the verification of anything; when there is, precisely, no longer enough philosophy to underpin any relationship between theory and practice; and when there is, precisely, no longer enough history to back up any historical proof of what happened.

We forget a little too easily that the whole of our reality is filtered through the media, including tragic events of the past. This means that it is too late to verify and understand those events historically, for the characteristic thing about the present period, the present *fin de siècle*, is the fact that the tools required for such intelligibility have been lost. History should have been understood while history still existed. Heidegger should have been denounced (or defended) while it was still possible to do so. A prosecution can be mounted only if a sequential continuum exists between the supposed crime and the trial. But we have now been transplanted elsewhere, and it is simply too late, as the television programme *Holocaust*, and even the film *Shoah*, clearly demonstrated. These things were not understood while we still had the means to understand them. Now they never will be. They never will be because such basic notions as responsibility, objective causes, or the meaning of history (or lack thereof) have disappeared, or are in the process of disappearing. The moral or social conscience is now a phenomenon entirely governed by the media, and the therapeutic zeal applied to its resuscitation is itself an index of how little wind it has left.

We shall never know now whether Nazism, the concentration camps or Hiroshima were intelligible or not: we are no longer part of the same mental universe. Victim and executioner are interchangeable, responsibility is diffrangible, dissoluble – such are the virtues of our marvellous interface. We no longer have the strength that forgetting gives: our amnesia is an amnesia of the image. Since everyone is guilty, who will declare an amnesty? As for autopsy, no one believes any longer in the anatomical accuracy of the facts: we have only models to work on. Even supposing the facts lay shining bright before our eyes, they would still not have the power to prove or convince. Consider how continual scrutiny of Nazism, of the gas chambers and so on, has merely rendered them less and less comprehensible, so that it has eventually become logical to ask an incredible question: 'But, in the last reckoning, did all those things really exist?' The question is perhaps an intolerable one, but the interesting thing here is what it is that makes it logically possible. And in fact what makes it possible is the media's way of replacing any event, any idea, any history, with any other, with the result that the more we scrutinize the facts, the more carefully we study details with a view to identifying causes, the greater is the tendency for them to cease to exist, and to cease to *have existed*. Confusion over the identity of things is thus a function of our very attempts to substantiate them, to fix them in memory. This indifference of memory, this indifference to history, is proportional to our efforts to achieve historical objectivity. One day we shall be asking ourselves whether Heidegger himself ever existed. The paradox of Robert Faurisson's thesis may seem repugnant – and indeed, it is repugnant in its *historical* claim that the gas chambers never existed – but at the same time it is a perfect reflection of a whole culture: here is the dead end of a *fin de siècle* so mesmerized by the horror of the century's origins that forgetting is an impossibility for it, and the only way out is denial.

So proof is useless, since there is no longer any historical discourse in which to frame the case for the prosecution, but punishment too is in any case an impossibility. Auschwitz and the final solution simply cannot be expiated. Punishment and crime have no common measure here, and the unrealistic character of the punishment ensures the unreality of the facts. What we are currently experiencing is something else entirely. What is actually occurring – collectively, confusedly, via all the trials and debates – is a transition from the historical stage to a mythical stage: the mythic – and media-led – reconstruction of all these events. And in a sense this mythic conversion is the only possible way, not to exculpate us morally, but to absolve us in phantasy from the guilt of this primal crime. But in order for this to be achieved, in order for even a crime to become a myth, the historical reality must first be eradicated. Otherwise, since all these things (fascism, the camps, the extermination) have been, and remain, historically unresolvable for us, we should be obliged to repeat them for ever like a primal scene. It is not nostalgia for fascism that is dangerous: what is dangerous – albeit pitiful – is that pathological re-enactment of the past in which everyone plays a part, in which everyone effectively collaborates – those who deny the existence of the gas chambers just as much as those who believe in their reality, Heidegger's detractors just as much as his defenders; what is dangerous is the mass delusion whereby all the wealth of imagination missing from our time, all the capital of violence and reality, now become illusory, is transplanted back to that time by a sort of compulsion to relive it, by a sort of deep-seated guilt over not having been there. All this bespeaks a desperate process of abreaction in response to the fact that these events are on the point of escaping us on the level of reality. The Heidegger affair, the Klaus Barbie trial, and so on, are just so many feeble convulsive reactions to this loss of reality – which is now *our reality*. Faurisson's claims are a cynical transposition of this loss of reality into the past. The statement 'It never existed' means simply that we ourselves no longer exist sufficiently even to sustain a memory, and that hallucinations are the only way we have left to feel alive.

POSTSCRIPT

In view of this, perhaps we ought simply to dispense with our present *fin de siècle*? I would suggest that the 1990s be abolished in advance, and that we go directly from 1989 to 2000. After all, the *fin de siècle* has already arrived, complete with its necro-cultural pathos, its endless commemorations and mummifications. Is there any good reason why we should have to languish for another decade in this hellish atmosphere?

RECTIFICATION: HIP, HIP, HOORAY!
HISTORY IS RISEN FROM THE DEAD!

The great event of the end of the century is under way! Everybody is suddenly breathing free at the idea that History, momentarily smothered under the weight of totalitarian ideology, has resumed its course with renewed vigour following the lifting of the blockade around the countries of Eastern Europe.

The field of History has supposedly at last been reopened to the unpredictable interplay of peoples and their thirst for freedom. In contrast to the depressive mythology of past *fins de siècle*, the end of the twentieth century is now supposed to inaugurate a dazzling remobilization of the final process, a rebirth of hope and a return to play of all possibilities.

On closer inspection, however, the event in question turns out to be rather more mysterious, rather more of an unidentified 'historical' object. The thawing out of the countries of the East is without doubt an extraordinary turn of events. But what exactly happens to freedom when it is defrosted? Such an operation must be a hazardous one, its outcome uncertain (quite apart from the fact that you are not supposed to refreeze what you have once defrosted). The USSR and the Eastern bloc constituted not just a deep-freeze for freedom but also a laboratory, an experimental environment in which freedom was isolated and subjected to very high pressures. The West, on the other hand, is merely a museum – or, more accurately, a dump – for freedom and the Rights of Man. If deep-freezing was the distinctive (and negative) mark of the Eastern universe, the ultra-fluidity of our Western universe is even more disreputable, because thanks to the liberation and liberalization of our mores and beliefs, the problem of freedom can simply no longer be posed. Rather, it is virtually resolved. In the West, freedom – the Idea of freedom – has died its fine death; all the recent commemorations have clearly shown that the idea of freedom is gone. In the East it has been murdered – but there is no such thing as the perfect crime. From an experimental standpoint it will be most interesting to see what freedom is like when it resurfaces, resuscitated after being stripped of all its signs. We should then get a sense of what such reanimation and postmortem rehabilitation can do. Freedom defrosted may not, after all, be so fair to look upon. And what if we find that it seeks nothing so much as to barter itself away in a fervent embrace of automobiles and kitchen appliances, even of mind-bending drugs and pornography: that is, to exchange itself immediately for Western liquid assets; to pass from the end of history by means of freezing to the end of history by means of ultra-fluidity, by means of circulation? Because the fascinating thing about the events in the East is certainly not that they may be seen as placidly coming to the aid of ailing democracy and supplying it with fresh energy (not to say fresh markets); what is far more fascinating is to observe the telescoping of two specific scenarios of the end of History: the scenario whereby it is frozen solid, as in the concentration camps, and the scenario according to which it comes to an end thanks to a total centrifugal expansion of communication. Both cases embody a final solution. And it is not impossible that the thawing out of human rights in the East may be the socialist equivalent to the 'depressurizing of the West': a simple dissipation into the Western void of the energies bottled up in the East for the last half-century.

The fervour accompanying these events may be deceptive. If it expresses nothing more than the zeal with which the countries of the East are casting aside the bonds of ideology, or if it is a mimetic fervour – a tribute, as it were, to those liberal countries where all liberty has already been traded in for a technically easy life – then we shall have found out definitively what freedom is worth, and that it is probably never to be discovered a second time. History offers no second helpings. On the other hand, it could be that the present thaw in the East may be as disastrous in the long term as the excess of carbon dioxide in the upper atmosphere, that it may bring about a political greenhouse effect, and so overheat human relations on the planet that the melting of the Communist ice-sheet will cause Western seaboards to be submerged. Odd that we should be in such absolute fear of the melting of the polar ice, and look upon it as a climatic catastrophe, while we aspire with every democratic bone in our bodies to the occurrence of just such an event on the political plane.

If in the old days the USSR had released its gold reserves onto the world market, that market would have been completely destabilized. Today, by putting back into circulation their vast accumulated store of freedom, the Eastern countries could quite easily destabilize that very fragile balance of Western values which strives to ensure that freedom no longer emerges as action but only as a virtual and consensual form of interaction; no longer as a drama but merely as the universal psychodrama of liberalism. A sudden infusion of freedom as a real currency, as violent and active transcendence, as Idea, would be in every way catastrophic for our present air-conditioned redistribution of values. Yet this is precisely what we are asking of the East: freedom, the image of freedom, in exchange for the material signs of freedom. This is an absolutely diabolical contract, by virtue of which one signatory is in danger of losing their soul, and the other of losing their creature comforts. But perhaps – who knows? – this may, after all, be the best thing for both sides.

Those societies that were formerly masked – Communist societies – have been unmasked. What is their face like? As for us, we dropped the mask long ago and have for a long time been without either mask or face. We are also without memory. We have reached the point of searching the water for signs of a memory that has left no traces, hoping against hope that something might remain when even the water's molecular memory has faded away. So it goes for our freedom: we would be hard put to it to produce a single sign of it, and we have been reduced to postulating its infinitesimal, intangible, undetectable existence in a (programmatic, operational) environment so highly dilute that in truth only a spectre of freedom floats there still, in a memory every bit as evanescent as water's.

The fountainhead of freedom in the West has run so dry (witness the commemoration of the French Revolution) that we can but put all our hopes in the East's reserves, as newly discovered and opened up. But once this store of freedom has been liberated (the Idea of Liberty having indeed become as scarce as a natural resource), what can be expected to happen except, as in any marketplace, the release of an intense but superficial energy generated by exchange, followed by a rapid collapse of differential energies and of prices?

What is the meaning of glasnost? A transparently clear reverse run through all the signs of modernity, but in speeded-up motion and at second hand (a postmodern remake, almost, of our original version of modernity); further-more, positive and negative signs are mixed up together here, so that human rights emerge side by side with crimes, catastrophes and accidents – all of which have taken an enthusiastic statistical leap in the USSR since the regime was liberalized. The country has even rediscovered pornography and extra-terrestrials – hitherto censored, but now celebrating their reappearance along with everything else. This is what lends the present global thaw its experimen-tal aspect: we see that crimes and catastrophes, be they nuclear or natural – everything, in fact, that has been repressed – are all part and parcel of human rights (religion too, naturally, along with fashion in the broadest possible sense) – and all this is a fine lesson in democracy. For everything that we are, all the supposedly universal signs of the human, we now observe resurgent in the East in the form of a kind of ideal hallucination, a kind of return of the repressed embracing the worst, the most trivial and the most worn-out features of Western 'culture' – which from now on knows no frontiers. The present conjuncture is thus a moment of truth for this culture, as was its earlier confrontation with the primitive cultures of the entire world (a confrontation from which the West can scarcely be said to have emerged with flying colours). Such is the irony of fate that it is we who are going to be obliged perhaps one day to save the historical memory of Stalinism, once the Eastern countries have forgotten all about it. In that case it will be up to us to put the memory of the dictator into cold storage, just as he once did to the movement of History itself; after all, the Stalinist big freeze is also part of our universal heritage.

There is another sense, too, in which these events are extraordinary. Those who adopt a self-righteous hostility to the idea of the end of History would do well to consider the turn History is now taking – as witness these current developments – not only towards its end (which remains part of the phantasy of a linear history) but at the same time in the direction of its systematic reversal and elimination. We are in the process of wiping out the whole of the twentieth century. We are wiping out all signs of the Cold War one by one, perhaps even all the signs of World War II and those of all the century's political and ideological revolutions. The reunification of Germany and many other things are inevitable, not in the sense of a leap forward of History but in the sense of a reverse rewriting of the whole of the twentieth century – a rewriting that will surely take up a very great deal of the century's last decade. At our present rate, we should soon be back to the Holy Roman–Germanic Empire. Here, perhaps, is the illumination we may expect for the present *fin de siècle*, and the true meaning of the much-debated phrase 'the end of History'. The fact is that we are busy, in accordance with an oddly enthusiastic mourning process, smoothing out the salient events of the century, white-washing the century, as though all that had occurred therein (revolutions, partitions of the globe, extermination, the violent transnationalism of states, or nuclear cliffhanging) – in short, History itself in its modern stage – amounted to nothing but an imbroglio with no exit, and as though everyone had now begun to unmake this history with an ardour equal in every way to that applied earlier to its making. Restoration, regression, rehabilitation, the revival of old frontiers, differences, specificities and religious beliefs – and everywhere, even on the level of social mores, the change of heart: apparently all the marks of liberation won over the last century are now fading, and perhaps they are all destined to disappear altogether one after the other. We are in the midst of an immense process of *revisionism*, but not in an ideological sense: History itself is what we are revising, and we seem anxious to finish the job before the end of the century. Do we perhaps nurture the secret hope that with the coming of the new millennium we might be able to start all over again with a clean slate? That somehow we can restore everything to its original state? But when exactly did that state exist? Before the twentieth century? Before the French Revolution? How far can this process of reabsorption and smoothing out take us? It can certainly occur very, very quickly – witness the events in the East. This is precisely because there is no construction involved, but rather a massive deconstruction of History which has assumed almost viral and epidemic proportions. Maybe after all the year 2000 will never occur, as I speculated long ago, for the simple reason that the curve of History will have become so accentuated as to create a reverse trajectory, with the result that that temporal horizon will never be attained. History would in that case turn out to have been an asymptote: an infinite curved line tending towards its own end, yet never reaching that end, and at the last moment veering off from it in the opposite direction.

THE FATE OF ENERGY

All the events described here are susceptible to two kinds of diagnosis: physical and metaphysical. From the physical point of view, we are apparently dealing with a sort of massive phase transition in a human system in disequilibrium. As with physical systems proper, this phase transition remains largely mysterious for us, but the catastrophic development in question is in itself neither beneficial nor malignant: it is simply catastrophic, in the literal sense of the word.

The prototype of this chaotic declination, of this hypersensitivity to initial conditions, is the fate of energy. Our culture has seen the development of the liberation of energy as an irreversible process. All previous cultures have depended on a reversible pact with the world, on a stable ordering of things in which energy release certainly played a role, but never on the liberation of energy as a basic principle. For us, energy is the first thing to be 'liberated', and all subsequent forms of liberation are founded on this model. Man himself is liberated as an energy source, so becoming the motor of a history and of a speeding-up of that history.

Energy is a sort of phantasy projection which nourishes all modernity's industrial and technical dreams; energy is also what tends to give our conception of man the sense of a dynamics of the will. We know, however, thanks to the most recent findings of modern physics on the phenomena of turbulence, chaos and catastrophe, that any flow – indeed, any linear process – when it is speeded up is inflected in a curious way, a way that produces catastrophe.

The catastrophe that lies in wait for us is not connected to a depletion of resources. Energy itself, in all its forms, will become more and more abundant (at any rate, within the broadest time frame that could conceivably concern us as humans). Nuclear energy is inexhaustible, as are solar energy, the force of the tides, of the great fluxes of nature, and indeed of natural catastrophes, earthquakes and volcanoes (and technological imagination may be relied on to find ways and means to harness them). What is alarming, by contrast, is the dynamics of disequilibrium, the uncontrollability of the energy system itself, which is capable of getting out of hand in deadly fashion in very short order. We have already had a few spectacular demonstrations of the consequences of the liberation of nuclear energy (Hiroshima, Chernobyl), but it must be remembered that any chain reaction at all, viral or radioactive, has catastrophic potential. Our degree of protection from pandemics is epitomized by the utterly useless glacis that often surrounds nuclear power stations. It is not impossible that the whole system of world-transformation through energy has already entered a virulent and epidemic stage corresponding to the most essential character of energy itself: a fall, a differential, an imbalance – a catastrophe in miniature which to begin with has positive effects but which, once overtaken by its own impetus, assumes the dimensions of a global catastrophe.

Energy may be looked upon as a cause which produces effects, but it is also an effect which is self-reproducing, and can thus cease to obey any law of causality. The paradox of energy is that it implies a revolution on the level of causes and a revolution on the level of effects – each, practically speaking, independent of the other. It thus becomes the locus not only of a chain of causes but also of an unhindered flood of effects.

Energy thus enters a state of superfusion. The whole system of world-transformation enters a state of superfusion. Formerly a material and productive variable, energy has now become a vertiginous process feeding upon itself (which is, incidentally, why there is no danger that we shall run out of it).

Consider New York City. It is a miracle that everything starts afresh each morning, considering how much energy has been used up the day before. The phenomenon is indeed inexplicable until one realizes that no rational principle of energy loss is at work here, and that the functioning of a megalopolis such as New York contradicts the second law of thermodynamics: the city feeds on its own hubbub, its own waste, its own carbon-dioxide emissions – energy arising from the expenditure of energy, thanks to a sort of miracle of substitution. Experts who base their calculations solely on the quantitative aspects of an energy system inevitably underestimate the peculiar energy source contributed by energy discharge itself. In the case of New York this discharge is completely spectacularized – supercharged by its own image. In *The Supermale*, Alfred Jarry describes a superfused energy of this order in connection with sexual activity, but it may also occur in the cases of mental and mechanical energy: as Jarry's *quintuplette* crosses Siberia in the wake of the Trans-Siberian, some velocipedists die, yet carry on cycling. *Rigor mortis* is replaced by *mobilitas mortis*, and the dead rider pedals on indefinitely, even accelerating, as a function of inertia. The energy released is boosted by the inertia of the dead.

Here we are reminded of Mandeville's *Fable of the Bees*, according to which the splendour of a society derives from its vices, its ills, its excesses and its shortcomings. This thesis is diametrically opposed to the economists' claim that if something is expended, it must obviously be produced. On the contrary, the more we spend, the more energy and wealth increase. The energy in question is, precisely, that of catastrophe – an energy that economic calculations can never take into account. A particular kind of exaltation familiar in mental processes is now to be encountered in material processes as well. All these considerations are quite unintelligible in terms of equivalence: they can be understood only in the context of reversibility and inordinacy.

Thus the energy of New Yorkers flows from their fouled air, from their speeded-up pace of life, from the panic and asphyxia created by their unimaginably inhuman environment. It is even quite probable that drugs, and all the compulsive activities that drugs bring in their train, also contribute to the level of vitality and crudely metabolic vigour of the city. Everything plays a part – from the most refined activities to the most degraded: a total chain reaction. Any notion of normal functioning has evaporated. All beings conspire (as one might have said in the eighteenth century) in the same excess, the same dramatic overexcitement, which, leaving the need to live far behind, has much more to do with an unreal obsession with survival – with that glacial passion for survival which seizes hold of everyone and feeds off its own ferocity.

To try to wean New Yorkers away from their extravagance and wastefulness, or to get them to slow the inhuman rhythm at which they live, would be mistaken on two counts. In the first place, they do not find their activity exhausting, though it would be for normal people: on the contrary, they draw an abnormal energy from it. Secondly, it would be humiliating for them if they were obliged to slow down and economize on their energy flow; this would represent a lowering of their collective status and compromise their claim to an immoderation and urban mobility which are without equal in the world and of which they all partake, whether consciously or unconsciously.

The dangers threatening the human species are thus less risks of *default* (exhaustion of natural resources, dilapidation of the environment, etc.) than risks of *excess*: runaway energy flows, chain reactions, or frenzied autonomous developments. This distinction is a vital one, for while risks of default can be addressed by a New Political Ecology, the basic assumptions of which are by now generally accepted (indeed, they are already written into the International Rights of the Species), there is absolutely nothing to counter this other immanent logic, this speeding-up of everything, which plays double or nothing with nature. In the first case, the restoration of equilibrium to our ecological niche is still possible, the energies in play could still be rebalanced; in the second case, however, we are confronted by a development that is irretrievably out of balance. In the first case ethical principles may be brought to bear: a teleology that transcends the material process involved – even if merely the goal of survival – may come into play; in the second case, however, a process whose only goal is limitless proliferation will inevitably absorb all transcendence and devour all agents thereof. A full-blown and planet-wide schizophrenia, therefore, now rules: even as all sorts of ecological measures are being taken, even as a strategy for the proper use of the world, for an ideal interaction with the world, is being deployed, there is a simultaneous prolifer-ation of enterprises of destruction, a total unleashing of the performance principle. And the very same forces often contribute to both trends.

Furthermore, though the end-point of the first tendency seems fairly clear – to wit, the saving of our species by means of ecological conviviality – we know absolutely nothing about the secret destination of the second. But surely this acceleration, this excentric motion, must have an end, must imply a *destiny* for the human species, a different symbolic relationship with the world that is much more complex and ambiguous than a relationship of balance and interaction? This too would be a vital destination – but it would involve a total risk.

If such a destination has indeed been chosen for us, it is obvious that ecology's rational deities will be powerless against the throwing of technology and energy into the struggle for an unpredictable goal, in a sort of Great Game whose rules are unknown to us. Even now we have no protection against the perverse effects of security, control and crime-prevention measures. We already know to what dangerous extremities we are led by prophylaxis in every sphere: social, medical, economic or political. In the name of the highest possible degree of security, an *endemic* terror may well be instituted that is in every way as dangerous as the *epidemic* threat of catastrophe. One thing is certain: in view of the complexity of the initial conditions and the potential reversibility of all the effects, we should entertain no illusions about the effectiveness of any kind of rational intervention. In the face of a process which so far surpasses the individual or collective will of the players, we have no choice but to accept that any distinction between good and evil (and by extension here any possibility of assessing the 'right level' of technological development) can have the slightest validity only within the tiny marginal sphere contributed by our rational model. Inside these bounds, ethical reflection and practical determinations are feasible; beyond them, at the level of the overall process which we have ourselves set in motion, but which from now on marches on independently of us with the ineluctability of a natural catastrophe, there reigns – for better or worse – the *inseparability of good and evil*, and hence the impossibility of mobilizing the one without the other. This is, properly speaking, the *theorem of the accursed share*. There is no point whatsoever in wondering whether things ought to be thus: they simply *are* thus, and to fail to acknowledge it is to fall utterly prey to illusion. None of this invalidates whatever may be possible in the ethical, ecological or economic sphere of our life – but it does totally relativize the impact of such efforts upon the symbolic level, which is the level of destiny.

THE THEOREM OF THE ACCURSED SHARE

The uninterrupted production of positivity has a terrifying consequence. Whereas negativity engenders crisis and critique, hyperbolic positivity for its part engenders catastrophe, for it is incapable of distilling crisis and criticism in homeopathic doses. Any structure that hunts down, expels or exorcizes its negative elements risks a catastrophe caused by a thoroughgoing backlash, just as any organism that hunts down and eliminates its germs, bacteria, parasites or other biological antagonists risks metastasis and cancer – in other words, it is threatened by a voracious positivity of its own cells, or, in the viral context, by the prospect of being devoured by its own – now unemployed – antibodies.

Anything that purges the accursed share in itself signs its own death warrant. This is the theorem of the accursed share.

The energy of the accursed share, and its violence, are expressions of the principle of Evil. Beneath the transparency of the consensus lies the opacity of evil – the tenacity, obsessiveness and irreducibility of the evil whose contrary energy is at work everywhere: in the malfunctioning of things, in viral attacks, in the acceleration of processes and in their wildly chaotic effects, in the overriding of causes, in excess and paradox, in radical foreignness, in strange attractors, in linkless chains of events.

The principle of Evil is not a moral principle but rather a principle of instability and vertigo, a principle of complexity and foreignness, a principle of seduction, a principle of incompatibility, antagonism and irreducibility. It is not a death principle – far from it. It is a vital principle of disjunction. Since the Garden of Eden, which Evil's advent closed to us, Evil has been the principle of knowledge. But if indeed we were chased from the Garden for the sin of knowledge, we may as well draw the maximum benefit from it. Trying to redeem the accursed share or the principle of Evil can result only in the establishment of new artificial paradises, those of the consensus, which for their part do indeed embody a true death principle.

To analyse present-day systems in their catastrophic reality, to consider not only their failures and aporias but also the way in which they sometimes succeed only too well and get lost in the delusion of their own functioning, is to come face to face at every turn with the theorem or equation of the accursed share, and to find its indestructible symbolic power confirmed every time.

Going over to the side of the principle of Evil implies making a choice in every sphere that is not only critical but also criminal. In any society, even a liberal one (such as ours!), this kind of choice cannot be publicly expressed. A stated position in support of the non-human or of the principle of Evil will be rejected by any value system (by 'principle of Evil' here I mean nothing more than the simple stating of a few hard truths concerning values, law, power, reality, etc.). In this respect there is no difference at all between East, West, North or South. And there is not the slightest chance of seeing an end to this intolerant attitude, as opaque and crystalline as a glass wall, which no progress in the sphere of either morality or immorality has managed to modify.

The world is so full of positive feelings, naive sentimentality, self-important rectitude and sycophancy that irony, mockery and the *subjective* energy of

evil are always in the weaker position. At this rate every last negative senti-
ment will soon be forced into a clandestine existence. Already the merest gibe
tends to meet with incomprehension. It will soon be impossible to express
reservations about anything at all. We shall have nothing left but disgust and
consternation.

Fortunately, the evil genie has taken up residence in *things*: this is the
objective energy of evil. No matter how we choose to describe whatever it is that
seeks thus to find a way forward – the accursed share, or strange attractors,
destiny, or a hypersensitive response to initial conditions – we shall not be able
to avoid its ever-increasing strength, its exponential trajectory or the veritable
pataphysics of incommensurable effects that it will generate. The excentric
development of our systems is ineluctable. As Hegel put it, we are amid 'the
life, moving of itself, of that which is dead'. Once certain limits have been
passed there is no relationship between cause and effect, merely viral relationships between one effect and another, and the whole system is driven by
inertia alone. The development of this increase in strength, this velocity and
ferocity of what is dead, is the modern history of the accursed share. It is not up
to us to explain this: rather, we must be its mirror in real time. We must outpace
events, which themselves long ago outpaced liberation. The reign of incoher-
ence, anomaly and catastrophe must be acknowledged, as must the vitality of
all those extreme phenomena which toy with extermination while at the same
time answering to certain mysterious rules.

It is in the nature of Evil, as it is in the nature of the accursed share, that it
regenerates in proportion as it is expended. Economically speaking this is
outrageous, much as the inseparability of Good and Evil can be outrageous
from a metaphysical point of view. But if violence is thus done to reason, we
must nevertheless acknowledge the vitality of this violence, the vitality of an
unforeseeable inordinacy which carries things beyond their original goals and
makes them hyperdependent on other ultimate ends (but which?).

All liberation affects Good and Evil equally. The liberation of morals and minds entails crimes and catastrophes. The liberation of law and pleasure leads inevitably to the liberation of crime (something which Sade understood well – and for that he has never been forgiven).

In the USSR perestroika has been characterized not only by ethnic and political demands but also by a surge of accidents and natural catastrophes (including crimes and accidents of the past, now disinterred). A kind of spontaneous terrorism has emerged in response to liberalization and the extension of human rights. All this, we are told, was already there – but censored. (One of the most deeply felt criticisms directed against the former Stalinist regime is that it deprived us of the many bloody events it censored, thus rendering them useless save as part of a political unconscious to be inherited by future generations; that it froze or deep-froze the titillating and bloodcurdling details of these crimes; and that, like the Nazis in the case of the Holocaust (another almost perfect crime), it *flouted the universal law of information.*

But there is more to this phenomenon than the lifting of censorship: the fact is that crime, delinquency and catastrophe rush towards the screen of glasnost like flies towards artificial light (why, incidentally, are flies never attracted to natural light?). This catastrophic surplus-value arises from an enthusiasm, almost a passion, on the part of nature, and equally from a spontaneous propensity of technology to indulge its own whims as soon as the political conditions are ripe. Frozen out for so long, crimes and catastrophes thus make their joyous and official entrance. If they did not exist they would have to be invented, for there can be no question that they are ultimately the true signs of freedom and the natural disorder of the world.

The totality constituted by Good and Evil together transcends us, but we should accept it totally. There can be no intelligence of things so long as this fundamental rule is ignored. The illusion that the two can be distinguished in order to promote one or the other is absurd. (This applies to the proponents of evil for evil's sake as much as to anyone else, for they will end up doing good.)

All kinds of events are out there, impossible to predict. They have already occurred, or are just about to heave into view. All we can do is train our searchlight, as it were, and keep our telescopic lens on this virtual world in the hope that some of those events will be obliging enough to allow themselves to be captured. Theory can be no more than this: a trap set in the hope that reality will be naive enough to fall into it.

The essential thing is to point the searchlight the right way. Unfortunately, we don't know which way that is. We can only comb the sky. In most instances the events are so far away, metaphysically speaking, that they merely cause a slight phosphorescence on the screen. They have to be developed and enlarged, like photographs. Not in order to discover their meaning, however: they are not logograms, but holograms. They can no more be *explained* than the fixed spectrum of a star or the variations of red.

To capture such strange events, theory itself must be remade as something strange: as a perfect crime, or as a strange attractor.

PART II

RADICAL OTHERNESS

*The Medusa represents an otherness so radical that one cannot look
at her and live.*

THE HELL OF THE SAME

Of all the prostheses that punctuate the history of the body, the double is doubtless the most ancient. The double, however, is not properly speaking a prosthesis at all. Rather, it is an imaginary figure, like the soul, the shadow or the mirror-image, which haunts the subject as his 'other', causing him to be himself while at the same time never seeming like himself. The double haunts the subject like a subtle death, but a death forever being conjured away. Things are not always like this, however – for when the double materializes, when it becomes visible, it signifies imminent death.

In other words, the double's imaginary power and resonance – the level upon which the subject's simultaneous estrangement from himself and intimacy with himself are played out – depends upon its lack of material being, upon the fact that the double is and remains a phantasy. Everyone may dream – and everyone no doubt does dream all his life long – of a perfect duplicate, or perfect multiple copies, of his own being; but the strength of such copies lies precisely in their dream quality, and is lost as soon as any attempt is made to force dream into reality. The same is true of the (primal) scene of seduction, which is effective only so long as it is a phantasy, something re-remembered – so long as it is never real. Ours is the only period ever to have sought to exorcize this phantasy (along with others) – that is, to turn it into flesh and blood, to transform the operation of the double from a subtle interplay involving death and the Other into the bland eternity of the Same.

Clones. Cloning. The piping of humans *ad infinitum*, based on the fact that any cell of an individuated organism may become the matrix of an identical individual. A child is reported to have been born in the United States after the fashion of a geranium – grown from a single cell taken from a single individual: from a 'father', the sole genitor, of whom this offspring was a perfect replica or twin.

The dream, then, of an eternal twinning as replacement for sexual procreation, with its link to death. A cellular dream of scissiparity – the purest form of parenthood in that it allows us at last to dispense with the other and go directly from the one to the same. This is a unicellular utopia which, thanks to genetics, gives complex beings access to the fate of the protozoans.

What, if not a death drive, would impel sexual beings towards a presexual form of reproduction (in the depths of our imagination, moreover, is it not precisely this scissiparous form of reproduction and proliferation based solely on contiguity that for us *is* death and the death drive?). And what, if not a death drive, would further impel us at the same time, on the metaphysical plane, to deny all otherness, to shun any alteration in the Same, and to seek nothing beyond the perpetuation of an identity, nothing but the transparency of a genetic inscription no longer subject even to the vicissitudes of procreation?

But enough of the death drive. Are we faced here with a phantasy of self-genesis? No, because such phantasies always involve the figures of the mother and the father – *sexed* parental figures whom the subject may indeed yearn to eliminate, the better to usurp their positions, but this in no sense implies contesting the symbolic structure of procreation: if you become your own child, you are still the child of someone. Cloning, on the other hand, radically eliminates not only the mother but also the father, for it eliminates the interaction between his genes and the mother's, the imbrication of the parents' differences, and above all the *joint* act of procreation.

The cloner does not beget himself: he sprouts from each of his genes' segments. One may well speculate about the value of such plant-like shoots, which in effect resolve all Oedipal sexuality in favour of a 'non-human' sex, a sex based on contiguity and unmediated propagation. But at all events the phantasy of self-genesis is definitively out of the picture. Father and mother are gone, but their disappearance, far from widening an aleatory freedom for the subject, instead leaves the way clear for a *matrix known as a code*. No more mother, no more father: just a matrix. And it is this matrix, this genetic code, which is destined to 'give birth', from now till eternity, in an operational mode from which all chance sexual elements have been expunged.

The subject, too, is gone, because identical duplication ends the division that constitutes him. The mirror stage is abolished by the cloning process – or, perhaps more accurately, is monstrously parodied therein. For the same reason cloning keeps nothing of the timeless narcissistic dream of the subject's projection into an ideal alter ego, for this projection too works by means of an image – the image in the mirror, in which the subject becomes alienated in order to rediscover himself, or that seductive and mortal image in which the subject recognizes himself as a prelude to his death. Nothing of all this is left with cloning. No more mediations – no more images: an individual product on the conveyor belt is in no sense a *reflection* of the next (albeit identical) product in line. The one is never a mirage, whether ideal or mortal, of the other: they can only accumulate, and if that is so it is precisely because they have not been sexually engendered and are unacquainted with death.

We are even beyond the realm of germination here, because true twins have their own specificity as such, and enshrine the particular, and sacrosanct, fascination of the Two – of that which has been two from the start, and has never been One. The only thing cloning enshrines, by contrast, is the reiteration of the same: 1 + 1 + 1 + 1, etc.

A clone is not a child, not a twin, not a narcissistic reflection; rather, it is the materialization of a double by genetic means – in other words, the abolition of all otherness and of the entire imaginary sphere.

A gene segment has no more need of an imaginary mediation in order to reproduce than does an earthworm, any segment of which can reproduce autonomously as an entire worm. Any cell of an American chief executive officer likewise suffices to produce a new chief executive officer. Similarly, any portion of a hologram may become the matrix of a new complete hologram: each discrete portion of the original hologram contains all the information needed for reproduction (though a slight loss of definition may occur).

This is how the totality is eliminated. If all information is contained in each of its parts, the whole loses its significance. This means the end of the body also, the end of that unique object which we call the body, whose secret is precisely that it cannot be broken down into an accumulation of cells because it is an indivisible configuration – as witness the very fact that it is sexed. Paradoxically, cloning is destined to continue producing sexed beings indefinitely – clones must, of course, remain identical to their model – even as it turns sex itself into a useless function; not that sex was ever a *function*: on the contrary, it is what makes a body a body, something which transcends all that body's diverse functions. Sex (or death) is something that transcends the entirety of the information that can be collected concerning a given body. The genetic formula, by contrast, contains all such information, but cannot transcend it. It must therefore find its own autonomous path to reproduction, independently of sexuality and death.

By breaking the body down into organs and functions, bio-physio-anatom-ical science had already begun a process of analytical dissection of which micromolecular genetics is merely a logical extension, though at a much higher level of abstraction and simulation: at the nuclear level of the command cell – directly at the level of the genetic code. And it is around genetics that this whole phantasmagoria is organized.

The functional and mechanist view still treated each bodily organ as a partial and differentiated prosthesis: simulation was already part of the picture, but simulation of a 'traditional' kind. In the view of cybernetics and computer science, by contrast, it is the smallest undifferentiated element, it is each cell of the body, which becomes an 'embryonic' prosthesis for that body. The genetic formula inscribed in each cell becomes the true modern prosthesis for all bodies. A prosthesis, as normally understood, is an artifact which replaces a defective organ, or an instrumental extension of the body; a DNA molecule, however, which stores all information relative to a given body, is the ultimate prosthesis in that it allows this body *to be extended ad infinitum by itself* – 'itself' being nothing more, now, than this infinite series of prostheses.

This cybernetic prosthesis is infinitely subtler, and more artificial, than any mechanical one. For the genetic code has nothing 'natural' about it. Any part abstracted from a whole and achieving autonomy from it becomes an artificial prosthesis which alters that whole because it replaces it (an idea contained in the etymology, *'pros + thesis'*). Similarly, the genetic code – which, inasmuch as it holds all the 'information' on a particular being, is in effect a condensation of the whole of that being – may be described as an artifact, an abstract matrix from which identical beings obeying identical commands will emerge, not through reproduction but by virtue merely of a kind of lease-renewal. (This is what makes genetic simulation so incredibly violent.)

My genetic inheritance was determined once and for all when a particular sperm encountered a particular ovum. This inheritance includes the formula of all the biochemical processes that brought me into being and ensure my functioning. A copy of this formula is written into each and every one of the tens of billions of cells of which I am at present composed. Each of these cells knows how to manufacture me; before being a cell of my liver or my blood, every cell is a cell of me. It is therefore theoretically possible to manufacture an individual identical to me from any one of them. (A. Jacquard)

Cloning is thus the last stage in the history of the modelling of the body – the stage at which the individual, having been reduced to his abstract and genetic formula, is destined for serial propagation. It is worth recalling in this context what Walter Benjamin had to say about the work of art in the age of its mechanical reproduction. What is lost when a work is massively reproduced is that work's 'aura', its unique here-and-now quality, its aesthetic form; at the same time the work fated to reproduction in this manner assumes a *political* form, according to Benjamin. What is lost is the original – which only a history that is itself nostalgic and retrospective can restore in its 'authenticity'. The most advanced, most modern form of this development – which Benjamin described in connection with contemporary cinema, photography and mass media – is that form where the original no longer even exists, because the objects in question are conceived of from the outset in terms of their limitless reproduction.

With the advent of cloning, this kind of thing is occurring not just at the level of messages but also in terms of individuals. Indeed, this is exactly what happens to the body when it is conceived of as nothing more than a message, nothing more than computer fodder. In such circumstances there is no obstacle in the way of a mass reproduction of the body exactly comparable to the mass reproduction of industrial objects and mass-media images described by Benjamin. Thus reproduction precedes production, and the genetic model of the body precedes all possible bodies. An exploding technology is what presides over this reversal – that technology which Benjamin was already able to describe, in its ultimate consequences, as a total medium; but Benjamin was writing in the industrial era: by then technology itself was a gigantic prosthesis governing the generation of identical *objects* and *images* which there was no longer any way of distinguishing from one another, but it was as yet impossible to foresee the technological sophistication of our own era, which has made it possible to generate identical *beings*, without any means of returning to an original. The prostheses of the industrial era were still external, *exotechnical*, whereas those we know now are ramified and internalized – *esotechnical*. Ours is the age of soft technologies, the age of genetic and mental software.

So long as the prostheses of the old industrial golden age were merely mechanical, they continued to have a retroactive effect upon the body, modifying its image; inversely, they were themselves metabolized on the imaginary level, and in their metabolized form became an integrated technological aspect of the body image. But there is a point of no return in simulation: the point when prostheses are introduced at a deeper level, when they are so completely internalized that they infiltrate the anonymous and micromolecular core of the body, when they impose themselves upon the body itself as the body's 'original' model, burning out all subsequent symbolic circuits in such a way that every possible body is now nothing but an invariant reproduction of the prosthesis: and this point means the end of the body, the end of its history, the end of its vicissitudes. It means that the individual is now nothing but a cancerous metastasis of his basic formula. How could all individuals cloned from individual X be anything more than a cancerous metastasis – the propagation of a single cell such as may be observed in cancer? There is a close connection between the key concept of the genetic code and the pathology of cancer. Cancer implies an infinite proliferation of a basic cell in complete disregard of the laws governing the organism as a whole. Similarly, in cloning, all obstacles to the extension of the reign of the Same are removed; nothing inhibits the proliferation of a single matrix. Formerly sexual reproduction constituted a barrier, but now at last it has become possible to isolate the genetic matrix of identity; consequently it will be possible to eliminate all the differences that have hitherto made individuals charming in their unpredictability.

If all cells are conceived of primarily as receptacles for a sole genetic formula, then what are they – not only all identical individuals, but also all the cells of a single individual – but the cancerous extension of that basic formula? A process of metastasis that began with industrial products has ended in the organization of cells. It is hardly worth asking whether cancer is a malady of the capitalist era, for it is so clearly the disease which dominates the whole of modern pathology. Cancer is the *form* of the virulence of the code: aggravated redundancy of the same signals – aggravated redundancy of the same cells.

The body-as-scene changes in accordance with the irreversible 'progress' of technology, and it is its overall scheme that undergoes metamorphosis. Prostheses of the traditional kind, designed to replace defective organs, change nothing so far as the general model of the body is concerned. The same applies to organ grafts. But what of the mental shaping of the body caused by psychotropic agents and drugs? It is the *body-as-scene* that is changed in this way. The body under the influence of psychotropic agents is a body modelled 'from within', a body that is no longer subject to the perspectivist space of representation, of mirrors and of discourse. A body silent, mental, already molecular (no longer specular); a body metabolized directly, without mediation of act or look; a body immanent to itself, deprived of otherness, of contextualization, of transcendence; a body abandoned to the implosive metabolic vagaries of cerebral and endocrine flows; a sensory body, but not a sensitive one, because it is connected up internally only – not to objects of perception (which is why it may be imprisoned in a 'blank' or void sensory world by simply disconnecting it from its *own* sensory nerve-endings and without altering anything in the outside world); a body that is already homogeneous, having reached a state of tactile plasticity, mental pliability and susceptibility to psychotropic influences, from whatever direction they might come, that is not far removed from nuclear and genetic manipulation – not far, that is, from the absolute loss of the body image, from the condition of bodies which cannot be represented at all, either for others or for themselves, the condition of bodies enucleated of their being and meaning by virtue either of transfiguration into a genetic formula or of biochemical influences: bodies definitively removed from any possibility of resurrection.

We no longer practise incest, but we have generalized it in all its derivative forms. The difference is that our version of incest is no longer sexual and familial, but rather scissiparous and protozoan. This is how we have got round the prohibition: by subdividing the Same, through a copulation between One and the Same unmediated by the Other. This is still incest, but without the tragedy. All the same, by giving material form – indeed, its most vulgar form – to this dangerous phantasy we have thereby also given material form to the curse that attends it, to the original repulsion and disgust, which are now on the increase in our societies as a function of the spread of this incestuous situation. Perhaps even the hell of other people would have been preferable to this return to the original form of an impossible kind of exchange.

Inasmuch as the individual no longer confronts the other, he finds himself face to face with himself. On account of an aggressive backlash on the part of his immune system, a dislocation of his own code and the destruction of his own defences, the individual becomes in a sense an antibody to himself. Our society is entirely dedicated to neutralizing otherness, to destroying the other as a natural point of reference in a vast flood of aseptic communication and interaction, of illusory exchange and contact. By dint of communication, our society develops an allergy to itself. By becoming transparent in its genetic, biological and cybernetic being, the body even develops an allergy to its own shadow. Otherness denied becomes a spectre and returns in the form of a self-destructive process. This, too, is the transparency of Evil.

Alienation is no more: the Other as gaze, the Other as mirror, the Other as opacity – all are gone. Henceforward it is the transparency of others that represents absolute danger. Without the Other as mirror, as reflecting surface, consciousness of self is threatened with irradiation in the void.

The utopia of the end of alienation has likewise disappeared. The subject has not succeeded in negating himself as subject, within the framework of a totalization of the world. A determinate negation of the subject no longer exists: all that remains is a lack of determinacy as to the position of the subject and the position of the other. Abandoned to this indeterminacy, the subject is neither the one nor the other – he is merely the Same. Division has been replaced by mere propagation. And whereas the other may always conceal a second other, the Same never conceals anything but itself. This is our clone-ideal today: a subject purged of the other, deprived of its divided character and doomed to self-metastasis, to pure repetition.

No longer the hell of other people, but the hell of the Same.

Two brothers live in a castle. Each has a daughter, and the two daughters are the same age. Both are sent away to school until they are eighteen. In the carriage bringing them home, one of the cousins is suddenly taken ill and dies. At the same moment, in the castle where he is awaiting her return, her father also dies. So only one of the girls arrives home alive, and there her father undresses her and offends nature by possessing her. At that very instant father and daughter are levitated in the bedchamber, fly out through a window and proceed to float above the surrounding countryside, petrified in their never-ending incestuous embrace. The passing over of the unnaturally entwined couple, flying without wings, sets up long negative vibrations which deeply affect everything that lives in the harmonious countryside below. A general disequilibrium, confused panic and an indefinable fear take over everywhere, and things degenerate to the point where humans commit acts contrary to reason, animals fall victim to illness and violent behaviour, and plants are filled with anxiety. All relationships are disturbed. (Guido Ceronetti)

THE MELODRAMA
OF DIFFERENCE

So what became of otherness?

We are engaged in an orgy of discovery, exploration and 'invention' of the Other. An orgy of differences. We are procurers of encounter, pimps of interfacing and interactivity. Once we get beyond the mirror of alienation (beyond the mirror stage that was the joy of our childhood), structural differences multiply *ad infinitum* – in fashion, in mores, in culture. Crude otherness, hard otherness – the othernesses of race, of madness, of poverty – are done with. Otherness, like everything else, has fallen under the law of the market, the law of supply and demand. It has become a rare item – hence its immensely high value on the psychological stock exchange, on the structural stock exchange. Hence too the intensity of the ubiquitous simulation of the Other. This is particularly striking in science fiction, where the chief question is always 'What is the Other? Where is the Other?' Of course science fiction is merely a reflection of our everyday universe, which is in thrall to a wild speculation on – almost a black market in – otherness and difference. A

veritable obsession with ecology extends from Indian reservations to house-
hold pets (otherness degree zero!) – not to mention the other of 'the other
scene', or the other of the unconscious (our last symbolic capital, and one we
had better look after, because reserves are not limitless). Our sources of
otherness are indeed running out; we have exhausted the Other as raw
material. (According to Claude Gilbert, we are so desperate that we go digging
through the rubble of earthquakes and catastrophes.)

Consequently the other is all of a sudden no longer there to be exterminated, hated, rejected or seduced, but instead to be understood, liberated,
coddled, recognized. In addition to the Rights of Man, we now also need the
Rights of the Other. In a way we already have these, in the shape of a universal
Right to be Different. For the orgy is also an orgy of political and psychological
comprehension of the other – even to the point of resurrecting the other in places
where the other is no longer to be found. Where the Other was, there has the
Same come to be.

And where there is no longer anything, there the Other *must* come to be.
We are no longer living the drama of otherness. We are living the psychodrama
of otherness, just as we are living the psychodrama of 'sociality', the psychodrama of sexuality, the psychodrama of the body – and the melodrama of all
the above, courtesy of analytic metadiscourses. Otherness has become socio-
dramatic, semiodramatic, melodramatic.

All we do in psychodrama – the psychodrama of contacts, of psychological
tests, of interfacing – is acrobatically simulate and dramatize the absence of
the other. Not only is otherness absent everywhere in this artificial drama-
turgy, but the subject has also quietly become indifferent to his own subjectivity,to his own alienation, just as the modern political animal has become
indifferent to his own political opinions. This subject becomes transparent,
spectral (to borrow Marc Guillaume's word) – and hence interactive. For in
interactivity the subject is the other to no one. Inasmuch as he is indifferent to
himself, it is as though he had been reified alive – but without his double,

without his shadow, without his other. Having paid this price, the subject becomes a candidate for all possible combinations, all possible connections.

The interactive being is therefore born not through a new form of exchange but through the disappearance of the social, the disappearance of otherness. This being is the other after the death of the Other – not the same other at all: the other that results from the denial of the Other.

The only interaction involved, in reality, belongs to the medium alone: to the machine become invisible. Mechanical automata still played on the difference between man and machine, and on the charm of this difference – something with which today's interactive and simulating automata are no longer concerned. Man and machine have become isomorphic and indifferent to each other: neither is other to the other.

The computer has no other. That is why the computer is not intelligent. Intelligence comes to us from the other – always. That is why computers perform so well. Champions of mental arithmetic and *idiots savants* are autistic – minds for which the other does not exist and which, for that very reason, are endowed with strange powers. This is the strength, too, of the integrated circuit (the power of thought-transference might also be considered in this connection). Such is the power of abstraction. Machines work more quickly because they are unlinked to any otherness. Networks connect them up to one another like an immense umbilical cord joining one intelligence and its twin. Homeostasis between one and the same: all otherness has been confiscated by the machine.

Does otherness survive anywhere after being banished from this entire psychodramatic superstructure?

Is there a physics as well as a metaphysics of the Other? Is there a dual, not just a dialectical, form of otherness? Is there still a form of the Other as destiny, and not merely as a psychological or social partner of convenience?

These days everything is described in terms of difference, but otherness is not the same thing as difference. One might even say that difference is what destroys otherness. When language is broken down into a set of differences, when meaning is reduced to nothing more than differentiation, the radical otherness of language is abolished. The duel that lies at the heart of language – the duel between language and meaning, between language and the person who speaks it – is halted. And everything in language that is irreducible to mediation, articulation or meaning is eliminated – everything, that is, which causes language at its most radical level to be *other* than the subject (and also Other to the subject?). The existence of this level accounts for the play in language, for its appeal in its materiality, for its susceptibility to chance; and it is what makes language not just a set of trivial differences, as it is in the eyes of structural analysis, but, symbolically speaking, truly a matter of life and death.

What, then, does it mean to say that women are the other for men, that the mad are the other for the sane, or that primitive people are the other for civilized people? One might as well go on for ever wondering who is the other for whom. Is the Master the slave's other? Yes, certainly – in terms of class and power relations. But this account is reductionistic. In reality, things are just not so simple. The way in which beings and things relate to each other is not a matter of structural difference. The symbolic order implies dual and complex forms that are not dependent on the distinction between ego and other. The Pariah is not the other to the Brahmin: rather, *their destinies are different.* The two are not differentiated along a single scale of values: rather, they are mutually reinforcing aspects of an immutable order, parts of a reversible cycle like the cycle of day and night. Do we say that the night is the other to the day? No. So why should we say that the masculine is the other to the feminine? For the two are undoubtedly merely reversible moments, like night and day, following upon one other and changing places with one another in an endless process of seduction. One sex is thus never the other for the other sex, except within the context of a differentialistic theory of sexuality – which is basically nothing but a utopia. *For difference is itself a utopia*: the idea that such pairs of terms can be split up is a dream – and the idea of subsequently reuniting them is another. (This also goes for the distinction between Good and Evil: the notion that they might be separated out from one another is pure fantasy, and it is even more utopian to think in terms of reconciling them.) Only in the distinction-based perspective of our culture is it possible to speak of the Other in connection with sex. Genuine sexuality, for its part, is 'exotic' (in Segalen's meaning of the term): it resides in the radical incomparability of the sexes – otherwise seduction would never be possible, and there would be nothing but alienation of one sex by the other.

Differences mean regulated exchange. But what is it that introduces disorder into exchange? What is it that cannot be negotiated over? What is it that has no place in the contract, or in the structural interaction of differences?

What is founded on the impossibility of exchange?

Wherever exchange is impossible, what we encounter is terror. Any radical otherness at all is thus the epicentre of a terror: the terror that such otherness holds, by virtue of its very existence, for the normal world. And the terror that this world exercises upon that otherness in order to annihilate it.

Over recent centuries all forms of violent otherness have been incorporated, willingly or under threat of force, into a discourse of difference which simulta-neously implies inclusion and exclusion, recognition and discrimination. Childhood, lunacy, death, primitive societies – all have been categorized, integrated and absorbed as parts of a universal harmony. Madness, once its exclusionary status had been revoked, was caught up in the far subtler toils of psychology. The dead, as soon as they were recognized in their identity as such, were banished to outlying cemeteries – kept at such a distance that the face of death itself was lost. As for Indians, their right to exist was no sooner accorded them than they were confined to reservations. These are the vicissi-tudes of a logic of difference.

Racism does not exist so long as the other remains Other, so long as the Stranger remains foreign. It comes into existence when the other becomes merely different – that is to say, dangerously similar. This is the moment when the inclination to keep the other at a distance comes into being.

'We may assume', wrote Victor Segalen, 'that fundamental differences will never resolve themselves into a truly seamless and unpatched fabric; increas-ing unity, falling barriers and great reductions in real distance must of themselves compensate somewhere by means of new partitions and unantici-pated gaps.'

Racism is one such 'new partition'. An abreaction to the psychodrama of difference: a response to the phantasy of – and obsession with – becoming 'other'. A way out of the psychodrama of perpetual introjection and rejection of the other. So intolerable is this introjection of differences, in fact, that the other must be exorcized at all costs by making the differences materially manifest. The biological claims of racism are without foundation but, by making the racial reference clear, racism does reveal the logical temptation at the heart of every structural system: the temptation to fetishize difference. But differential systems can never achieve equilibrium: differences oscillate con-stantly between absolute highs and absolute lows. When it comes to the management of otherness and difference, the idea of a well-tempered balance is strictly utopian.

Inasmuch as the humanist logic of difference is in some sense a universal simulation (one which culminates in the absurdity of a 'right to difference'), it leads directly, for all its benevolence, to that other desperate hallucination of difference known as racism. As differences and the cult of differences continue to grow, another, unprecedented kind of violence, anomalous and inaccessible to critical rationality, grows even faster. Segalen's 'unanticipated gaps' are not simply new differences: what springs up in order to combat the total homogenization of the world is the Alien – monstrous metaphor for the corpse-like, viral Other: the compound form of all the varieties of otherness done to death by our system.

This is a racism which, for lack of any biological underpinning, seizes on the very slightest variations in the order of signs; a racism which quickly takes on a viral and automatic character, and perpetuates itself while revelling in a generalized semiotics. And this racism can never be countered by any humanism of difference, for the simple reason that it is itself the virus of difference.

Sermonizing on the internalization of the other and the introjection of differences can never resolve the problem of the monstrous forms of otherness, because these forms are the product, precisely, of this selfsame obsessional differentiation, this selfsame obsessional dialectic of ego and other. Herein lies the whole weakness of those 'dialectical' theories of otherness which aspire to promote the proper use of difference. For if racism in its viral, immanent, current and definitive form proves anything, it is that there is no such thing as the proper use of difference.

This is why it may also be said that *the critique of racism is substantially finished* – just as Marx said that the critique of religion was substantially finished. Once the vacuousness of the metaphysical account of religion had been demonstrated, religion was supposed to disappear as the conditions of a more advanced mode of production became operative. Likewise, once the vacuousness of the biological theory of races has been demonstrated, racism is supposed to disappear as the conditions of a more advanced universal intermixture of differences become operative. But what if religion, for example, contrary to Marx's predictions, had lost its metaphysical and transcendent form only to become an immanent force and fragment into countless ideological and practical variants under the conditions of a religious revival drawing sustenance from the progress of the very social order that was expected to eradicate even the memory of religion? For the signs of just such a turn of events are all around us today. And much the same goes for racism, which has also become an immanent, viral and everyday reality. The fact is that the 'scientific' and rational critique of racism is a purely formal one, which demolishes the argument from biology but remains caught in the racist trap because it addresses a biological illusion only, and fails to deal with biology itself *qua* illusion. Similarly, the political and ideological critique of racism is purely formal in that it tackles the racist obsession with difference without tackling difference itself *qua* illusion. It thus itself becomes an illusion of criticism, bearing on nothing, and in the end racism turns out to have survived critique by rationalism just as deftly as religion survived critique by materialism – which is why all such critiques are indeed substantially finished.

There is no such thing as the proper use of difference – a fact revealed not only by racism itself but also by all anti-racist and humanitarian efforts to promote and protect differences. Humanitarian ecumenism, the ecumenism of differences, is in a cul-de-sac: the cul-de-sac of the concept of the universal itself. The most recent illustration of this, in France, was the brouhaha over the wearing of headscarves for religious reasons by North African schoolgirls. All the rational arguments mustered in this connection turned out to be nothing but hypocritical attempts to get rid of the simple fact that no solution is to be found in any moral or political theory of difference. It is difference itself that is a reversible illusion. We are the ones who brought difference to the four corners of the earth: that it should now be returned to us in unrecognizable, Islamic, fundamentalist and irreducible forms is no bad thing.

The guilt we feel in this connection assumes gigantic proportions. Not long ago the organization Médecins Sans Frontières became aware that the medical supplies it had been distributing in Afghanistan were being resold rather than used directly by their recipients. This precipitated a crisis of conscience for the programme's organizers. Should donations be discontinued, or should this immoral and irregular commerce be tolerated out of respect for 'cultural differences'? After much soul-searching it was decided to sacrifice Western values on the altar of difference, and continue to underwrite the black market in medicines. *Humanisme oblige*.

Another charming illustration of the confusion besetting our humanitarians concerns X, posted to the Sudan to study 'the communications needs of Sudanese peoples'. Seemingly, the Sudanese did not know how to communicate. But they were certainly hungry, and needed to learn how to grow sorghum. Sending agronomists being too expensive a prospect, the decision had been taken to teach by videocassette. The time had come for the Sudanese to join the communications revolution: sorghum via audio and video. No hook-up, no eat. It was not long before towns and villages were crammed with VCRs. A little longer, and the local mafia created a lucrative market for itself in pornographic videotapes which held a distinctly greater interest for the populace than educational cassettes on sorghum cultivation. Porno-Sorgho-Video: The Same Struggle!

The risibility of our altruistic 'understanding' is rivalled only by the profound contempt it is designed to conceal. For 'We respect the fact that you are different' read: 'You people who are underdeveloped would do well to hang on to this distinction because it is all you have left'. (The signs of folklore and poverty are excellent markers of difference.) Nothing could be more contemptuous – or more contemptible – than this attitude, which exemplifies the most radical form of incomprehension that exists. It has nothing to do, however, with what Segalen calls 'eternal incomprehensibility'. Rather, it is a product of eternal stupidity – of that stupidity which endures for ever in its essential arrogance, feeding on the differentness of other people.

Other cultures, meanwhile, have never laid claim to universality. Nor did they ever claim to be different – until difference was forcibly injected into them as part of a sort of cultural opium war. They live on the basis of their own singularity, their own exceptionality, on the irreducibility of their own rites and values. They find no comfort in the lethal illusion that all differences can be reconciled – an illusion that for them spells only annihilation.

To master the universal symbols of otherness and difference is to master the world. Those who conceptualize difference are anthropologically superior – naturally, because it is they who invented anthropology. And they have all the rights, because rights, too, are their invention. Those who do not conceptualize difference, who do not play the game of difference, must be exterminated. The Indians of America, when the Spanish landed, are a case in point. They understood nothing about difference; they inhabited radical otherness. (The Spaniards were not different in their eyes: they were simply gods, and that was that.) This is the reason for the fury with which the Spaniards set about destroying these peoples, a fury for which there was no religious justification, nor economic justification, nor any other kind of justification, except for the fact that the Indians were guilty of an absolute crime: their failure to under-stand difference. When they found themselves obliged to become part of an otherness no longer radical, but negotiable under the aegis of the universal concept, they preferred mass self-immolation – whence the fervour with which they, for their part, allowed themselves to die: a counterpart to the Spaniards' mad urge to kill. The Indians' strange collusion in their own extermination represented their only way of keeping the secret of otherness.

Cortés, the Jesuits, the missionaries and, later on, the anthropologists – even Tzvetan Todorov himself in his *Conquest of America* – all came down on the side of negotiable otherness. (Las Casas is the sole exception: towards the end of his life he suggested that the Conquest be purely and simply abandoned, and that the Indians be put back in the hands of their own destiny.) All these enlightened souls believe in a proper use of difference. The radical Other is intolerable: he cannot be exterminated, but he cannot be accepted either, so the negotiable other, the other of difference, has to be promoted. This is where a subtler form of extermination begins – a form involving all the humanist virtues of modernity.

An alternative account of the extermination is that the Indians had to be exterminated not because they were not Christians but because they were more Christian than the Christians themselves. Their cruelty and their human sacrifices were intolerable to the Spaniards not because they excited pity or moral indignation but because this cruelty bore witness to the authority of their gods and the strength of their beliefs. This force of conviction amongst the Indians made the Spaniards ashamed at how little religion they themselves had. It made a mockery of a Western culture which, behind its flimsy façade of faith, had no gods except gold and commerce. The Indians, with their implacable religiousness, made Western culture ashamed of its profanation of its own values. Their fanaticism was intolerable because it was an implicit condemnation and demystification of Western culture in its own eyes (the same role is being played today by Islam). This crime could not be expiated, and in itself sufficiently justified the extermination of its perpetrators.

It is by no means clear that the other exists for everyone. Does the other exist for the Savage or the Primitive? Some relationships are asymmetrical: the one may be the other for the other without this implying that the other is the other for the one. I may be other for him even though he is not the other for me.

The Alakaluf of Tierra del Fuego were wiped out without ever having sought to understand the Whites, without ever even speaking to them or negotiating with them. They called themselves 'Men' – and there were no others. In their eyes the Whites were not even different: they were unintelligible. They evinced no surprise at the newcomers' vast wealth and amazing technology. Despite three centuries of contact, the Alakaluf adopted not a single Western technique, continuing, for instance, to row around in skiffs. The Whites might oppress and slaughter them, but it was for all the world as if they did not exist. The Alakaluf were to be annihilated without conceding anything of their otherness. They would never be assimilated – indeed, they would never even reach the stage of difference. They would perish without ever allowing the Whites the privilege of recognizing them as different. The Alakaluf were simply irrecuperable. For the Whites, nevertheless, they were 'others' – beings that were different yet still human, or at least human enough to be evangelized, exploited, and killed.

As a sovereign people the Alakaluf called themselves 'Men'. Then the Whites applied to them the name that they had originally applied to the Whites: 'Foreigners'. They eventually came to refer to themselves as 'foreigners' in their own language. In later times they called themselves 'Alakaluf' – the only word that they still pronounced in front of Whites, meaning 'Give, give'. They thus ended up with a designation connoting the mendacity to which they had been reduced. First, then, they were themselves, then strangers to themselves, and finally absent from themselves: three names reflecting three stages of their extermination. Naturally their murder is to be attributed to those who possess the universalizing vision, those who manipulate otherness for their own profit. In their singularity, which could not even conceive of the Other, the Alakaluf were inevitably vanquished. But who can say that the elimination of this singularity will not turn out, in the long run, to be fatal for the Whites too? Who can say that radical foreignness will not have its revenge – that, though effectively conjured away by colonial humanism, it will not return in the form of a virus in the bloodstream of the Whites, dooming them to disappear themselves one day in much the same way as the Alakaluf.

Everything is subservient to the system, yet at the same time escapes its control. Those groups around the world who adopt the Western lifestyle never really identify with it, and indeed are secretly contemptuous of it. They remain excentric with respect to this value system. Their way of assimilating, of often being more fanatical in their observance of Western manners than Westerners themselves, has an obviously parodic, aping quality: they are engaged in a sort of *bricolage* with the broken bits and pieces of the Enlightenment, of 'progress'. Even when they negotiate or ally themselves with the West, they continue to believe that their own way is fundamentally the right one. Perhaps, like the Alakaluf, these groups will disappear without ever having taken the Whites seriously. (For our part we take *them* very seriously indeed, whether our aim is to assimilate them or destroy them: they are even fast becoming the crucial – negative – reference point of our whole value system.)

The Whites will perhaps themselves disappear one day without ever having understood that their whiteness is merely the result of the promiscuity and confusion of all races and cultures, just as the whiteness of white light is simply the resolution of the melodrama of all colours. And just as colours become comparable amongst themselves only when they are measured against a universal scale of wavelengths, so cultures become comparable only when they are set against a structural scale of differences. But there is a double standard here, for it is only for Western culture that other cultures are different. For those other cultures themselves, Whites are not even different – they are non-existent, phantoms from another world. Outward conversion to Western ways invariably conceals inward scoffing at Western hegemony. One is put in mind of those Dogons who made up dreams to humour their psychoanalysts and then offered these dreams to the analysts as gifts. Once we despised other cultures; now we respect them. They do not respect our culture, however; they feel nothing but an immense condescension for it. We may have won the right by conquest to exploit and subjugate these cultures, but they have offered themselves the luxury of mystifying us.

The strangest feeling one is left with after reading Bruce Chatwin's *Songlines* is a lingering perplexity about the reality of the 'lines' themselves: do these poetic and musical itineraries, these songs, this 'dreamtime', really exist or not? In all these accounts there is a hint of mystification; a kind of mythic optical illusion seems to be operating. It is as though the Aboriginals were fobbing us off. While unveiling the profoundest and most authentic of truths (the Austral myth at its most mysterious), they also play up the most modern and hypothetical of considerations: the irresolvability of any narrative, absolute doubt as to the origins. For us to believe these fabulous things, we need to feel that they themselves believe them. But these Aboriginals seem to take a mischievous pleasure in being allusive and evasive. They give a few clues, but never tell us the rules of the game, and one cannot help getting the impression that they are improvising, pandering to our phantasies, but withholding any reassurance that what they are telling us is true. This is doubtless their way of keeping their secrets while at the same time poking fun at us – for in the end we are the only people who want to believe these tales.

The Aboriginals' secret resides not in what they omit to say, however, but entirely within the thread, within the indecipherable filigree of the narrative; we are confronted by an ironic form here, by a mythology of appearances. And in the manipulation of this form the Aboriginals are far more adept than we are. We Whites are liable to remain mystified for a good while yet.

The simulation of Western values is universal once one gets beyond the boundaries of our culture. Is it not true, though, that in our heart of hearts we ourselves, who are neither Alakaluf nor Aboriginal, neither Dogon nor Arab, fail signally to take our own values seriously? Do we not embrace them with the same affectation and inner unconcern – and are we not ourselves equally unimpressed by all our shows of force, all our technological and ideological pretensions? Nevertheless, it will be a long time before the utopian abstraction of our universal vision of differences is demolished in our own eyes, whereas all other cultures have already given their own response – namely, universal indifference.

It is not even remotely a matter of rehabilitating the Aboriginals, or finding them a place in the chorus of human rights, for their revenge lies elsewhere. It lies in their power to destabilize Western rule. It lies in their phantom presence, their viral, spectral presence in the synapses of our brains, in the circuitry of our rocketship, as 'Alien'; in the way in which the Whites have caught the virus of origins, of Indianness, of Aboriginality, of Patagonicity. We murdered all this, but now it infects our blood, into which it has been inexorably transfused and infiltrated. The revenge of the colonized is in no sense the reappropriation by Indians or Aboriginals of their lands, privileges or autonomy: that is *our* victory. Rather, that revenge may be seen in the way in which the Whites have been mysteriously made aware of the disarray of their own culture, the way in which they have been overwhelmed by an ancestral torpor and are now succumbing little by little to the grip of 'dreamtime'. This reversal is a worldwide phenomenon. It is now becoming clear that *everything* we once thought dead and buried, everything we thought left behind for ever by the ineluctable march of universal progress, is not dead at all, but on the contrary likely to return – not as some archaic or nostalgic vestige (all our indefatigable museumification notwithstanding), but with a vehemence and a virulence that are modern in every sense – and to reach the very heart of our ultra-sophisticated but ultra-vulnerable systems, which it will easily convulse from within without mounting a frontal attack. Such is the destiny of radical otherness – a destiny that no homily of reconciliation and no apologia for difference is going to alter.

IRRECONCILABILITY

To the principle of conjunction and reconciliation stands opposed the principle of disjunction and irreconcilability. From this confrontation the principle of irreconcilability always emerges triumphant, because by definition it can never give way to the principle of reconciliation.

The same sort of thing happens in the case of Good and Evil. The Good consists in a dialectic of Good and Evil. Evil consists in the negation of this dialectic, in a radical dissociation of Good and Evil, and by extension in the autonomy of the principle of Evil. Whereas the Good presupposes a dialectical involvement of Evil, Evil is founded on itself alone, in pure incompatibility. Evil is thus master of the game, and it is the principle of Evil, the reign of eternal antagonism, that must eventually carry off the victory.

When it comes to radical otherness between beings, sexes or cultures, we find the same kind of antagonism as in the case of Evil, the same logic of definitive incomprehensibility, the same bias in favour of foreignness. Is it possible, then, to join forces with this foreignness? The answer is no, because of the theorem which may be advanced, by analogy with the behaviour of heavenly bodies, according to which bodies and minds are forever drawing farther and farther away from each other. This hypothesis of an endless process of excommunication, which subsumes the notion of an indissoluble curse, is also, precisely, the hypothesis of the transparency of Evil – as opposed to the universal utopia of communication. A hypothesis, therefore, that is everywhere contradicted by the facts. But only *apparently* so, for in reality the more things seem to become orientated towards universal comprehension and universal homogenization, the more unavoidable becomes the idea of an eternal irreducibility whose ineradicable presence is easier to sense than to analyse.

This presence imposes itself as the brute fact, as the irresistible, suprasensory, supranatural reality which is thrown up as a figure of fatality by the impossibility of a dialectical theory of difference. A kind of universal force of repulsion confronting the official universal force of attraction.

In its irreconcilability, this force is present in every culture. It is still at work today in the relationships between the Third World and the West, between Japan and the West, or between Europe and America, and also within each culture, in the shape of those deviant forms which eventually come to predominate. Morocco, Japan or Islam will *never* become Western. Europe will never bridge the gulf of modernity that separates it from America. Cosmopolitan evolutionism is an illusion, and it is everywhere being exposed as such.

There is no solution to Foreignness. It is eternal – and radical. It is not a matter of wanting it to be that way. It simply *is* so.

This is Radical Exoticism: the rule governing the world. It is not a law, for the law is the universal principle of understanding, the regulated interplay of differences, moral, political and economic rationality. It is a *rule* – and, like all rules, implies an arbitrary *predestination*. Consider languages, none of which is reducible to any other. Languages are predestined, each according to its own rules, its own arbitrary determinants, its own implacable logic. Each obeys the laws of communication and exchange, certainly, but at the same time it answers to an indestructible internal coherence; a language as such is, and must forever remain, fundamentally untranslatable into any other language. This explains why all languages are so 'beautiful' – precisely because they are foreign to one another.

A law is never ineluctable: it is a concept, founded upon a consensus. A rule, by contrast, is indeed ineluctable, because it is not a concept but a form that orders a game. Seduction illustrates this well. Eros is love – the force of attraction, of fusion, of conjunction. Seduction is the far more radical figure of disjunction, distraction, illusion and diversion, a figure that alters essence and meaning, alters identity and the subject. And, contrary to common belief, entropy is on the side not of universal disjunction but of conjunction and fusion, of love and understanding – on the side of the proper use of differences. Seduction – exoticism – is an excess of the other, of otherness, the vertiginous appeal of what is 'more different than different': this is what is irreducible – and this is the true source of energy.

In this predestined world of the Other, everything comes from elsewhere – happy or unhappy events, illnesses, even thoughts themselves. All imperatives flow from the non-human – from gods, beasts, spirits, magic. This is a universe of fatality, not of psychology. According to Julia Kristeva we become estranged from ourselves by internalizing the other, and this estrangement from ourselves takes the form – among others – of the unconscious. But in the world of fatality the unconscious does not exist. There is no universal form of the unconscious, as psychoanalysis claims, and the only alternative to unconscious repression is fatality – the imputation of everything to a completely non-human agency, an agency which is external to the human and delivers us from it.

The question of the Other in this fatal universe is the question of hospitality.

Hospitality represents a reciprocal, ritualized and theatrical dimension. Whom are we to receive, and how are we to receive them? What rules should we follow here? For we exist solely to be received, and to receive (not to be known and recognized). This symbolic dimension is precisely what is missing from communication, in which the message is merely decoded, never given or received. The message is passed – but there is no exchange between people. The abstract dimension of meaning is transmitted, while the aspect of reciprocity is short-circuited.

The Other is my guest. Not someone who is legally equal, though different; but a foreigner, a stranger, *extraneus*. And for this very reason, his strangeness has to be exorcized. But once he has been initiated in due form, my guest's life becomes even more precious to me than my own. In this symbolic universe there is no place for the otherness of difference. Neither animals, nor gods, nor the dead, are *other*. All are caught up in the same cycle. If you are outside the cycle, however, you do not even exist.

All other cultures are extraordinarily hospitable: their ability to absorb is phenomenal. Whereas we waver between the other as prey and the other as shadow, between predation pure and simple and an idealizing recognition, other cultures still retain the capacity to incorporate what comes to them from without, including what comes from our Western universe, into their own rules of the game. They may perform this recycling operation instantaneously or over the long term, but in no case are their code and basic arrangements threatened thereby. Precisely because they do not live by the illusion of a universal law, they are not rendered oversensitive as are we, who are constantly being commanded to internalize the law and to make ourselves the origin of our own selves, acts, tastes and pleasures. Primitive cultures do not burden themselves with pretensions of this order. Being oneself means nothing to them: everything comes from the Other. There is no such thing as oneself, nor is there any call for such a thing.

From this point of view there is not much difference between Japan and Brazil, or between either of them and Jean Rouch's 'manic priests': all are cannibals in the sense that they offer a lethal hospitality to values that are not and never will be theirs.

The strength of the Japanese lies in the kind of hospitality they accord to technology and to all forms of modernity (just as, in the past, they opened their doors to religion and writing). Their hospitality involves no psychological internalization or commitment on their part, however, and things are kept strictly at the level of codes. It is more a form of challenge than an offer of reconciliation or recognition: their own impenetrability remains total. This is, literally, a sort of seduction whereby something – a sign, a technique or an object – is diverted from its own essence and made to function in another code; or – to put it another way – made to pass from the realm of laws (capital, value, economy, meaning) into the realm of rules (play, rituals, ceremonies, cycles, repetition).

Japanese dynamism corresponds to neither the value system nor the goals of the Western project. Its practical applications manifest a distantiation and operational purity unencumbered by the ideologies and beliefs that have shaped the history of capital and technology in the West. The Japanese are the great play-actors of technology, unknowingly upholding in the sphere of technology the paradox of the actor in the theatre: the most effective actor must have detachment, he must have rules to go by, and his own inspiration must come from outside – from the role, or from the technical object, as the case may be. (Japanese industrialists believe that there is a god concealed within each product of technology, making it autonomous and infusing it with its own inner spirit.) Technology is to be played with as signs are played with: the subject should efface himself completely, meaning should be at its most elliptical – in short, pretence should be the order of the day.

Symbolic rituals can absorb anything, including the organless body of capitalism. They obviate any need to leave one's own ground, and involve neither Heideggerian speculation on technology's relationship to the origins and to being, nor psychological internalization. The Japanese challenge the West on its own terms, but their strategy is infinitely more effective: the strategy of a value system that can *afford the luxury of technology*, of a technological practice founded on pure artifice and having absolutely nothing to do with progress or similar rational forms. For us this pure strategy, this cold and painstaking efficiency, so different from the trivial modernity of the West, is an enigmatic and indeed unintelligible form. In this sense it is one of those forms that Segalen describes as radical exoticism, and one which is all the more startling in that it 'affects' the ways of an overdeveloped society while at the same time retaining all primitive society's power of ritual.

Japanese culture is thus a cannibalistic form – assimilating, absorbing, aping, devouring. Afro-Brazilian culture is also a rather good example of cannibalism in this sense: it too devours white modern culture, and it too is seductive in character. Cannibalism must indeed always be merely an extreme form of the relationship to the other, and this includes cannibalism in the relationship of love. Cannibalism is a radical form of hospitality.

This is not to say that the race question is any nearer resolution in Brazil than anywhere else – simply that racist ideology faces a more difficult task in Brazil on account of the racial confusion and the range of race mixtures that exist there. Discrimination confronts a web of racial lines as unpredictable as the lines of the human palm. This invalidation of racism by virtue of the scattering of its object is far more subtle and effective than ideological struggle, whose ambiguity invariably revives the very problem it seeks to resolve. Racism will never end so long as it is combated frontally in terms of rational rebuttal. It can be defeated only through an ironic give-and-take founded precisely on racial differences: not at all through the legitimation of differences by legal means, but through an ultimately violent interaction grounded in seduction and voracity. One thinks of the Bishop of Pernambuco; one thinks of the words 'How good he was, my little Frenchman!' He is very good-looking, so he is sanctified – and eaten. He is granted something greater than the right to exist: the prestige of dying. If racism is a violent abreaction in response to the Other's seductive power (rather than to the Other's difference), it can surely be defused only by an increase in seductiveness itself.

So many other cultures enjoy a more original situation than ours. For us everything is predictable: we have extraordinary analytical means but no situation to analyse. We live theoretically well beyond our own events: hence our deep melancholy. For others destiny still flickers: they live it, but it remains for them, in life as in death, something forever indecipherable. As for us, we have abolished 'elsewhere'. Cultures stranger than ours live in prostration (before the heavens, before destiny); we live in consternation (at the absence of destiny). Nothing can come from anywhere except from us. This is, in a way, the most absolute misfortune.

RADICAL EXOTICISM

The very scale of the efforts made to exterminate the Other is testimony to the Other's indestructibility, and by extension to the indestructible totality of Otherness.

Such is the power of this idea, and such is the power of the facts.

Radical otherness survives everything: conquest, racism, extermination, the virus of difference, the psychodrama of alienation. On the one hand, the Other is always-already dead; on the other hand, the Other is indestructible.

This is the Great Game.

The ultimate inscrutability of beings, as of peoples.

Segalen: 'The inscrutability of races, which is merely the extension to races of the inscrutability of individuals.'

The survival of exoticism depends entirely on the impossibility of encounter, fusion and the exchange of differences. Fortunately, all this is an illusion – the illusion of subjectivity itself.

All that endures is the foreignness of the foreigner, the irredeemability of the object.

No psychology: psychology is always the worst way to go.

Avoid all psychological, ideological and moral forms of the Other – eschew the metaphor of the Other, the Other as metaphor.

Seek the Other's 'cruelty', the Other's unintelligibility, the Other as spectre: constrain the Other to foreignness, violate the Other in his foreignness.

Running to ground of metaphor: sublime form of metaphorical violation.

Radical anti-ethnology, anti-universalism, anti-differentialism.

Radical exoticism versus the pimping of differences.

Segalen summed things up with regard to the discovery of the world and of other cultures: once the Earth had been circumscribed as a sphere, as a finite space, thanks to all-powerful means of communication, what remained was the inevitability of a circular tourism wearing itself out in the absorption of all differences, in the most trivial form of exoticism. Nevertheless, having identified this fatal entropy, this levelling of all cultures, and the consequent impossibility of travel, Segalen proceeds to revive the grand prospect of an Essential or Radical Exoticism.

> Exoticism is the acute and immediate perception of an eternal incomprehensibility.

What triumphs, then, is not the rule of difference and lack of differentiation but instead an eternal incomprehensibility, the irreducible foreignness of cultures, manners, faces, languages.

> If savour increases as a function of difference, what could be more savoury than the antagonism of irreducibles, the clash of eternal contrasts?

The irredeemability of the object: 'The essential exoticism is that which the Object has for the Subject.' Exoticism as the fundamental law of the intensity of sensations, of the exaltation of the senses, and thus of living itself . . .

'All men are subject to the law of exoticism.'

Is it really a law? Is the theory of exoticism ethical or aesthetic? Is it a philosophy, an art of living, a vision of the world? Is it impressionistic or doctrinal? For Segalen, it is an unavoidable hypothesis and a source of pleasure.

Radical otherness is simultaneously impossible to find and irreducible. Impossible to find as otherness *per se* (obviously a dream); but at the same time irreducible as a symbolic rule of the game, as a rule of the game that governs the world. The promiscuity and general confusion in which differences exist do not affect this rule of the game as such: it is not a rational law, nor is it a demonstrative process – we shall never have either metaphysical or scientific proof of this principle of foreignness and incomprehensibility: we simply have to accept it.

The worst thing here is understanding, which is sentimental and useless. True knowledge is knowledge of exactly what we can never understand in the other, knowledge of what it is in the other that makes the other not oneself – and hence someone who can in no sense become separated from oneself, nor alienated by any look of ours, nor instituted by us in either identity or difference. (Never question others about their identity. In the case of *America*, the question of American identity was never at issue: the issue was America's foreignness.) If we do not understand the savage, it is for the same reason that he does not understand himself (the term 'savage' conveys this foreignness better than all later euphemisms).

The rule of exoticism thus implies that one should not be fooled by understanding, by intimacy, by the country, by travel, by picturesqueness, or by oneself. The realm of radical exoticism, moreover, is not necessarily a function of travel: 'It is not essential, in order to feel the shock [of the exotic], to revive the old-fashioned episode of the voyage. [. . .] The fact remains that such an episode and its setting are better than any other subterfuge for reaching this brutal, rapid and pitiless hand-to-hand conflict and making each blow count.' Travel is a subterfuge, then – but it is the most appropriate one of all.

The power of the antipodes: the critical power of travel. The finest period of the Other: Jean de Lhéry, Montesquieu, Segalen.

It is the moment when otherness erupts that is sublime. The eighteenth century. The other must be maintained in his foreignness. Barthes and Japan. America. Try not to apprehend the other as difference. This is Segalen's principle of *l'Exote*. No pretension to truth. Disgust for trivial exoticism. At the same time, do not seek to abolish oneself in face of the other. That was Isabelle Eberhardt's temptation: fused form equals mystical confusion. Her response to the question 'How can one be an Arab?' was to try to become an Arab, by rejecting her own foreignness. It was inevitable that she should die as a result, and it was an Arab who cast her into the sea to erase her apostasy. Rimbaud, for his part, never sought fusion. His foreignness with respect to his own culture was too great for him to need any mystical diversion.

Patagonia. Phantasy of disappearance. The disappearance of the Indians, your own disappearance, that of all culture, all landscape, in the bleakness of your mists and ice. In essence, though, all these things are disappearing right here in Europe too: we are all Alakaluf. Why this geographical dispersion? The last word here is that it is better to put an end to a process of creeping disappearance (ours) by means of a live sojourn in a *visible* form of disappearance. All translations into action are imaginary solutions. That is why 'Patagonia' goes so well with 'Pataphysics', which is the science of imaginary solutions. Pataphysics and agonistics: Patagonistics.

What we seek in travel is neither discovery nor trade but rather a gentle deterritorialization: we want to be taken over by the journey – in other words, by absence. As our metal vectors transcend meridians, oceans and poles, absence takes on a fleshly quality. The clandestineness of the depths of private life gives way to annihilation by longitude and latitude. But in the end the body tires of not knowing where it is, even if the mind finds this absence exalting, as if it were a quality proper to itself.

Perhaps, after all, what we seek in others is the same gentle deterritorialization that we seek in travel. Instead of one's own desire, instead of discovery, we are tempted by exile in the desire of the other, or by the desire of the other as an ocean to cross. The looks and gestures of lovers already have the distance of exile about them; the language of lovers is an expatriation in words that are afraid to signify; and the bodies of lovers are a tender hologram to eye and hand, offering no resistance and hence susceptible of being crisscrossed, like airspace, by desire. We move around with circumspection on a mental planet of circumvolutions, and from our excesses and passions we bring back the same transparent memories as we do from our travels.

Travel is comparable to relationships with others. The voyage as metamorphosis, as anamorphosis, of the Earth. The feminine as metamorphosis and anamorphosis of the masculine. Transference as deliverance from one's own sex or one's own culture. It is this form of travel, founded on expulsion and deliverance, that has now taken the place of the classical voyage, the voyage of discovery. Travel today is spatial and orbital, vectored – the kind of travel which, by virtue of its speed, also plays with time. Such is the voyage in the Age of Aquarius: a voyage into versatility, into the reversibility of seasons and cultures. Escape from the illusion of intimacy.

Once the peripheral extension of a central activity, a diversion from an enduring place of origin, travel has all of a sudden changed its meaning: it now constitutes an original dimension, the dimension of no return, the new primal scene. It has thus become truly exotic – the future's answer to the former decentredness of primitive society. At the same time, whereas travel once served to confirm the increasing monotony of countries and peoples, the planet-wide levelling of cultures, and was pursued with the masochism that underlies the illusions of the tourist, travel now leads, by contrast, to radical exoticism, and serves to confirm the fundamental incompatibility of cultures.

Travel was once a means of being elsewhere, or of being nowhere. Today it is the only way we have of feeling that we are somewhere. At home, surrounded by information, by screens, I am no longer anywhere, but rather everywhere in the world at once, in the midst of a universal banality – a banality that is the same in every country. To arrive in a new city, or in a new language, is suddenly to find oneself here and nowhere else. The body rediscovers how to look. Delivered from images, it rediscovers the imagination.

What could be more closely bound up with travel, with the anamorphosis of travel, than photography? What could be closer to travel in its origins? Hence photography's affinity with everything that is savage and primitive, and with that most essential of exoticisms, the exoticism of the Object, of the Other.

The most beautiful of all photographs are those taken of savages in their natural surroundings. The savage is always confronting death, and he confronts the lens in exactly the same manner. He does not ham it up, nor is he indifferent. He always poses; he faces up to the camera. His achievement is to transform this technical operation into a face-to-face confrontation with death. This is what makes these pictures such powerful and intense photographic objects. As soon as the lens fails to capture this pose, this provocative obscenity of the object facing death, as soon as the subject begins to collude with the lens, and the photographer too becomes subjective, the 'great game' of photography is over. Exoticism is dead. Today it is very hard indeed to find a subject – or even an object – that does not collude with the camera lens.

The only trick here, generally speaking, is to be ignorant of how one's subjects live. This gives them a certain aura of mystery, a savagery, which the successful picture captures. It also captures a gleam of ingenuity, of fatality, in their faces, betraying the fact that they do not know who they are or how they live. A glow of impotence and awe that is completely lacking in our tribes of worldly, devious, fashion-conscious and self-regarding people, always well-versed in the subject of themselves – and hence devoid of all mystery. For such people the camera is merciless.

The only genuinely photographic subjects are those which are violated, taken by surprise, discovered or exposed despite themselves, those which should never have been represented because they have neither self-image nor self-consciousness. The savage – like the savage part of us – has no reflection. He is savagely foreign to himself. The most seductive women are the most self-estranged (Marilyn). Good photography does not represent anything: rather, it captures this non-representability, the otherness of that which is foreign to itself (to desire, to self-consciousness), the radical exoticism of the object.

Objects, like primitives, are way ahead of us in the photogenic stakes: they are free a priori of psychology and introspection, and hence retain all their seductive power before the camera.

Photography records the state of the world in our absence. The lens explores this absence; and it does so even in bodies and faces laden with emotion, with pathos. Consequently, the best photographs are photographs of beings for which the other does not exist, or no longer exists (primitives, the poor, objects). Only the non-human is photogenic. Only when this precondition is met does a kind of reciprocal wonder come into play – and hence a collusiveness on our part *vis-à-vis* the world, and a collusiveness on the part of the world with respect to us.

Photography is our exorcism. Primitive society had its masks, bourgeois society its mirrors, and we have our images.

We believe that we bend the world to our will by means of technology. In fact it is the world that imposes its will upon us with the aid of technology, and the surprise occasioned by this turning of the tables is considerable.

You think you are photographing a scene for the pleasure of it, but in fact it is the scene that *demands to be photographed*, and you are merely part of the décor in the pictorial order it dictates. The subject is no more than the funnel through which things in their irony make their appearance. The image is the ideal medium for the vast self-promotion campaign undertaken by the world and by objects – forcing our imagination into self-effacement, our passions into extraversion, and shattering the mirror which we hold out (hypocritically, moreover) in order to capture them.

The miraculous thing about the present period is that appearances, so long reduced to a voluntary servitude, have now become sovereign, and turned back towards (and against) us by means of the very technology from which we had earlier evicted them. Today they come from elsewhere, from their own place, from the heart of their banality, of their objectality: they surge forth on all sides, multiplying of their own accord, and joyfully. (The joy of taking photographs is an *objective* joy, and anyone who has never felt the objective transports of the image, some morning, in some town or desert, will never understand the pataphysical delicacy of the world.)

If a thing wants to be photographed, this is precisely because it does not want to offer up its meaning, because it does not want to have a reflection. It wants to be apprehended directly, violated on the spot, illuminated in detail under its fractal aspect. One can tell that a thing wants to be photographed, that it wants to become an image, and it is certainly not because it wants to endure: on the contrary, it wants to disappear. The human subject is a good photographic medium, moreover, only if he enters into the spirit of this game, if he suspends his own gaze and his own aesthetic judgement, if he takes pleasure in his own absence.

A photographic image must have this quality of a universe from which the subject has withdrawn. The very detail of the object, of line and light, should signify this suspension of the subject, and hence also of the world, which is what creates the photograph's tension. By means of the image the world imposes its discontinuity, its fragmentation, its distension, its artificial instantaneousness. From this standpoint the photograph is the purest of images, for it simulates neither time nor motion and is thus unrealistic in the strictest sense. All other kinds of images (cinema, etc.), far from being advances, are perhaps merely less thoroughgoing forms of that divorce of the pure image from reality. The intensity of the image is proportional to its discreteness and maximal abstraction – that is, to its bias towards the denial of reality. Creating an image consists in stripping the object of all its features one by one: weight, outline, feel, depth, time, continuity – and, of course, meaning. Only thanks to this disincarnation, to this exorcism, does the image acquire its extra fascination, its intensity; only thus does it become the conduit of pure objectality, permeable to a subtler kind of seduction. Restoring all these dimensions one after the other – outline, motion, emotion, idea, pathos, meaning, desire – as a way of doing better, of getting closer to reality (i.e. merely improved simulation) is a total nonsense where images are concerned. This is where technology falls into its own trap.

In photography, things are linked by a technical operation that corresponds to the way in which they are linked in their everyday banality. The fatal attraction of the object as perennial detail. The magical excentricity of the detail. What is an image for another image, a photo for another photo? Fractal contiguity, the absence of any dialectic: no 'world-view', no gaze – just the refraction of the world, of the world in its details, each with an equal chance.

The photographic image is dramatic. Dramatic by virtue of its silence. Dramatic by virtue of its immobility. What things dream of, what we dream of, is not motion but this more intense immobility. The force of the unmoving image: the force of the mythic opera. Even the cinema cultivates the myth of slow motion and the freeze-frame as moments of highest drama. And the paradoxical contribution of television may turn out to be the restoration of all its charm to the silence of the image.

The photographic image is dramatic, too, on account of the struggle it embodies between the subject's will to impose an order, a vision, and the object's will to impose itself in its discreteness and immediacy. If all goes well the object carries the day, for the photo-image is the image of a fractal world for which no formula, no summary, exists anywhere. In this it differs from art, from painting, even from the cinema – all of which inevitably strive, thanks to a concept, a vision or an internal movement, to limn the figure of a totality.

Not, then, the subject's detachment with respect to the world, but the disconnectedness of objects amongst themselves, the haphazard sequence of part-objects and details. Musical syncopation, or the motion of physical particles. Photography brings us closer than anything else to the fly, with its faceted eye and the broken line of its flight.

Perhaps the desire to take photographs arises from the observation that on the broadest view, from the standpoint of reason, the world is a great disappointment. In its details, however, and caught by surprise, the world always has a stunning clarity.

The secret form of the Other is what has to be reconstituted, as in anamorphosis, starting with the fragments and tracing its broken lines, its lines of fracture.

PURSUIT IN VENICE

A strange pride incites us not only to possess the other but also to force the other's secret out of him, not only to be dear to the other but also to be fatal to him. To play the *éminence grise* in the other's life.

You begin by following people at random, in the street, in short unorganized bursts, with the notion that people's lives are haphazard itineraries without meaning, heading nowhere – and fascinating for that very reason. You feel that you exist only when you are on their track – without their knowing it; in fact you are tracking yourself – without your knowing it. You are not really doing this, then, to discover how the other lives, nor where he is going; nor are you drifting in search of the unknown. Rather, you are allowing yourself to be seduced by being the other's mirror without his knowledge. By becoming his destiny, by repeating his itinerary – which, though it has a meaning for him, has none when you duplicate it. It is as though someone, behind him, knew that he was going nowhere. In a way, his goal has thus been stolen from him: an evil genie has slipped surreptitiously between him and his self. This effect is so powerful that people often sense that they are being followed; they have an intuition that something has entered their space and altered its geometry.

In Sophie Calle's *La Suite vénitienne*, S. decides one day to give an extra dimension to this experiment by following a man she barely knows throughout a trip he is making to Venice. She manages to locate the hotel where he is staying. She rents a room opposite so that she can observe his comings and goings. She photographs him continually. She wants nothing from him, has no desire to know him. Since he might recognize her, she disguises herself as a blonde. But Carnival holds no attraction for her, and she spends a fortnight surmounting endless difficulties in order to keep on the trail of her prey. She questions people in the shops he visits, she knows which shows he goes to. She even knows the exact time of his return to Paris, and goes to await his arrival so that she can take a last snapshot of him.

Does she want him to kill her? Does she want him to find her pursuit so intolerable (especially since she wants nothing out of it, least of all romance) that he will attack her physically or turn on her, like Orpheus on Eurydice, and make her disappear? Is she hoping that things will suddenly be reversed and that *he* will become *her* destiny? Like all games, this one too has its fundamental rule: nothing must happen that might facilitate a contact or a relationship between them. The secret must not be revealed, for fear of falling into banality.

Obviously there is something lethal here for the one who is being followed, and who must consequently try to wipe out his tracks as fast as he makes them. For one can no more live without leaving tracks than one can without casting a shadow. S., as his *éminence grise*, is stealing his tracks, and he cannot fail to sense the magic to which he is being subjected. He is being photographed incessantly. The photograph here has neither a voyeuristic nor an archival function. Its simple message has the form: at this location, at such and such a time, in this particular light, someone was present. But at the same time it conveys the following: there was no point in being here, in such and such a place, and at such and such a time – and in fact no one *was* here; I was the one who followed him, and I can assure you that no one was here.

It is of no interest to know that someone is leading a double life. It is *the tailing itself that supplies the other with a double life.* The most ordinary of lives may be transfigured in this way; likewise, the most extraordinary of lives may be rendered trite. In any case, life thus succumbs to a strange attraction.

We should not say 'The other exists, I have met him', but instead 'The other exists, I have followed him'. Meeting, confrontation, is always too real, too direct, too indiscreet. There is no secret involved. Think how people meeting each other are forever recognizing each other, forever reciting their identities (just as people who love each other are forever telling each other so). Can they be so sure of themselves? Does encountering the other really prove that he exists? Nothing could be more doubtful. On the other hand, if I follow the other secretly, he exists – precisely because I do not know him, because I do not want to know him, nor to have him recognize me. He exists because, without having chosen to, I exercise a deadly right over him: the right to follow. Without ever having approached him, I know him better than anyone. I can even leave him – as S. does in *La Suite vénitienne* – with the certitude that I shall find him again tomorrow in the labyrinth of the city in accordance with a sort of astral conjunction (because the city is curved, because space is curved, because the rules of the game inevitably put the two protagonists back on the same orbit).

The only way to avoid encountering someone is to follow him (according to a principle opposed to the principle of the labyrinth, where you follow someone so that you do not lose him). Implicit in the situation, however, is the dramatic moment when the one being followed, suddenly intuiting, suddenly becoming conscious that there is someone behind him, swings round and spots his pursuer. Then the rules are reversed, and the hunter becomes the hunted (for there is no escaping laterally). The only truly dramatic point is this unexpected turning-round of the other, who insists upon knowing and damns the consequences.

This reversal does in fact occur in the Venice scenario. The man comes towards her and asks her: 'What do you want?' She wants nothing. No mystery story, no love story. This answer is intolerable, and implies possible murder, possible death. Radical otherness always embodies the risk of death. S.'s anxiety revolves entirely around this violent revelation: the possibility of getting herself unmasked – the very thing she is trying to avoid. 'I cannot go on following him. He must be uneasy, he must be wondering if I am here, behind him – surely he is thinking about me now – so I shall have to keep track of him in some other way.'

S. could have met this man, seen him, spoken to him. But in that case she would never have produced this secret form of the existence of the Other. The Other is the one whose destiny one becomes, not by making his acquaintance in difference and dialogue but by entering into him as into something secret, something forever separate. Not by engaging in a conversation with him as interlocutor, but by entering into him as his shadow, as his double, as his image, by embracing the Other the better to wipe out his tracks, the better to strip him of his shadow. The Other is never the one with whom we *communicate*: he is the one whom we follow – and who follows us.

The other is never naturally the other: the other must be rendered other by being seduced, by being made alien to himself, even by being destroyed – if there is no alternative (but in fact there are subtler ways of achieving this end).

Each of us lives by setting traps for the other. The one and the other live in an endless affinity, an affinity which endures until prostration decides the issue. Everyone *wants* their other. Everyone has an imperious need to put the other at their mercy, along with a heady urge to make the other last as long as possible so as to savour him. The opposing logics of the lie and the truth unite in a dance of death which is nothing but pure delight at the other's demise. For desire for the other is always also the desire to put an end to the other (albeit, perhaps, at the latest possible moment?). The only question is which one will hold out the longest, occupying the space, the speech, the silence, the very inner world of the other – who is dispossessed of himself at the very moment when he becomes one in his difference. Not that one kills the other: the adversary is simply harassed into desiring, into willingly acceding to his own symbolic death . . . The world is a perfectly functioning trap.

An otherness, a foreignness, that is ultimately unintelligible – such is the secret of the form, and the singularity, of the emergence of the other.

> Yes, of course, *Ferdydurke* does show how individuals are determined by their environment, but what for me has far deeper implications for psychology, what is far more disturbing from a philosophical standpoint, is that on occasion a man can be created by another man, by another himself, by virtue of a fortuitous encounter, and at any moment . . . I am not concerned with pointing out that a particular social milieu can impose its conventions on me, or – as Marx would argue – that man is a product of his social class. What I want to show is the contact a man can have with his counterpart, and the immediate, fortuitous and wild character of this contact: to demonstrate how, on the basis of such a haphazard relationship, forms are brought into being that are absolutely unexpected, even absurd . . . Is it not obvious to you that a form of this kind is something far more powerful than a mere social convention? That this is an element which simply cannot be controlled?
>
> (Witold Gombrowicz)

VIRAL HOSPITALITY

Each of us is the destiny of the other, and no doubt the secret destiny of each of us is to destroy (or seduce) the other – not by virtue of a curse or some kind of death drive, but by virtue of our own vital destination.

It is perhaps not unreasonable to conceive of the evolution of an infectious disease within the human body by analogy with the history of a certain type of microbe, a history complete with beginning, climax and period of decline. A history which indeed parallels that of the human race: the dimensions differ, naturally, but from the point of view of the idea, the two are identical.

The type of microbe in question lives in the blood, the lymph, the tissues of a human individual. This human being, whom we think of as afflicted by disease, is the microbe's landscape, its world. And for these minuscule individuals, to strive unconsciously and involuntarily to destroy this world of theirs, and often to succeed in so doing, is the basic requirement and the entire meaning of their existence. (Who is to say that the different members of this race of microbes are not endowed, just as human individuals are, with greatly varying talents and wills, and that there are not among their number both ordinary microbes and geniuses?)

Might it not then be surmised that from the standpoint of some higher organism, humanity is itself a sickness; that the existence of humanity has this organism as prerequisite, as basic requirement, as meaning, and that we are forever striving – indeed, *obliged* – to destroy it progressively as we develop, just as the microbes strive to destroy a human individual 'afflicted by disease'? And, following this line of thought, is it not reasonable to suppose that the mission of any living community, be it a community of microbes or a community of human beings, is to destroy, little by little, a world that transcends it, whether that world is a human individual or our universe?

Even if this supposition were close to the truth, however, our imagination would still be at a loss to deal with it, for the human mind can grasp only downward, not upward, movements. We have relative knowledge only of what is at a lower elevation; when it comes to higher realities, we are confined to mere presentiments. We may perhaps, though, be permitted in this connection to interpret the history of humanity as an eternal struggle against the divine, which, despite its resistance, is gradually, and of necessity, being destroyed by the human. By extension we may speculate that this transcendent principle, which seems to us – or which we sense as – divine, is itself in turn transcended by another, even higher, principle, and so on *ad infinitum.*

(Arthur Schnitzler)

Between the race of microbes and the race of humans there exists a total symbiosis and a radical incompatibility. One cannot say that the microbe is other to man: the two are never opposed in their essential natures, and they do not confront one another in any real sense; they are linked together, however, and this interlinking is, as it were, predestined: no one (neither men nor bacilli) can imagine things being any other way. Nor is there any clear line of demarcation, because this link is reproduced over and over *ad infinitum.* So perhaps after all we shall have to conclude that otherness is located here: that the absolute Other is indeed the microbe in its radical non-humanness – a being of which we know nothing, and which cannot even be deemed *different* from us. The microbe as the hidden form which alters everything – and with which no negotiation or reconciliation is possible. Yet we are quickened by the same life as the microbe, and the race of microbes will perish along with the human race: we share the same destiny. One is reminded of the worm that has a sort of alga living in its stomach, without whose help it can digest no food. This is a fine arrangement until the day the worm takes a notion to devour the alga itself. And it does so – but dies as a result (without even digesting it, of course, because the alga is no longer there to help it to do so).

THE DECLINATION OF WILLS

The secret of the other is that it is never given to me to be myself, and that I exist only thanks to a fatal declination of something coming from elsewhere. In Schnitzler's apologia, man lives off the life of the species of microbe that has colonized him and is destined to destroy him: man and microbe are strangers to one another, but their destiny is shared. In *La Suite vénitienne*, S. does not know either what she is or where she is going: she follows someone who is going somewhere, and shares his secret without knowing it. It is thus always by virtue of a declination of meaning, or of non-meaning, that existence takes on form – by virtue, that is, of the deflection of something else. We have no will of our own, and the other is never what we would, of our own volition, choose to confront. Rather, the other is an invasion by something from elsewhere, priority given to what comes from elsewhere, seduction by foreignness and the transmission of foreignness.

So the secret of philosophy may not be to know oneself, nor to know where one is going, but rather to go where the other is going; not to dream oneself, but rather to dream what others dream; not to believe oneself, but rather to believe in those who do believe: to give priority to all determinants from elsewhere. Whether they are legible or not, decipherable or not, is of no consequence – the main thing is to embrace the foreign form of any event, any object, any fortuitous being, because in any case you will never know who you are. Today, when people have lost their shadows, it is of the utmost importance to be followed by someone; today, when everyone is losing their own tracks, it is of the utmost urgency that someone be on your tracks: even if he wipes them out and makes you disappear as a result, at least your disappearance will have occurred in a collusive mode; at least a symbolic form of obligation, an enigmatic form of conjunction and disjunction, will have been brought into play.

We live in a culture which strives to return to each of us full responsibility for his own life. The moral responsibility inherited from the Christian tradition has thus been augmented, with the help of the whole modern apparatus of information and communication, by the requirement that everyone should be answerable for every aspect of their lives. What this amounts to is an expulsion of the other, who has indeed become perfectly useless in the context of a programmed management of life, a regimen where everything conspires to buttress the autarky of the individual cell.

This, however, is an absurdity: no one can be expected to be entirely responsible for his own life. This Christian-cum-modern idea is futile and arrogant. It is also a utopian notion with no justification whatsoever. It requires that the individual should transform himself into a slave to his identity, his will, his responsibilities, his desire; and that he should start exercising control of all his own circuitry, as well as all the worldwide circuits that happen to cross paths within his genes, nerves or thought: a truly unheard-of servitude.

How much more human to place one's fate, one's desire and one's will in the hands of someone else. The result? A circulation of responsibility, a declination of wills, and a continual transferring of forms.

Inasmuch as my life is played out within the other, it becomes a mystery to itself. Inasmuch as my will is transferred to the other, it too becomes a mystery to itself.

There is always some doubt about the reality of our pleasure, about the strength of our will. Curiously, though we are never completely certain, the other's pleasure somehow seems less doubtful. Being closer to our own pleasure, we are better placed to cast doubt on it. To argue that everyone is inclined to give too much credit to his own opinion is to underestimate the contrary tendency: the subordination of one's own opinion to that of other people supposedly better equipped to hold opinions (this is rather like the Chinese erotic practice of postponing one's own pleasure to ensure that of the other, thus saving energy and gaining deeper knowledge). The hypothesis of the Other itself may perhaps be the consequence of this radical doubt of ours with respect to our own desire.

If it is true that seduction is founded upon my intuition of something in the other that remains forever secret for him, something that I can never know directly about him but which nevertheless exercises a fascination upon me from behind its veil of secrecy, then today there can be very little leeway left for seduction, for the other retains very little mystery for himself. The fact is that everyone is devilishly self-aware these days, devilishly conscious of the nature of their own desire. Everything is now so clear that the very fact of presenting oneself behind a mask is liable to elicit nothing but mockery. In such a context, what becomes of the poker game of seduction? Where, for that matter, is the illusion of desire – except, perhaps, in the theoretical illusion of psychoanalysis or the political illusion of revolution?

One may be no longer capable of belief, yet remain capable of believing in those who believe. One may be no longer capable of loving, except for loving someone who loves. One may no longer know what one wants, yet want what someone else wants. A kind of generalized derogation is occurring, whereby wish, ability and knowledge, though not forsaken, are being surrendered to another, a second agency. Already, in any case, the filter of screens, photographs, video images and news reporting allows us access only to that which has already been seen by others. We are indeed incapable of apprehending anything that has not already been seen. We have assigned machines the task of seeing for us – just as, before long, we shall assign computers the task of making all our decisions. All our functions, even organic and sensory ones, are relayed by satellite. A comparison may even be drawn with the mental division of pleasure: just as desire is not need, so pleasure is not satisfaction. Desire and pleasure *repose on* need and satisfaction, which are strategies of the above-mentioned second agency.

At all events, it is better to be controlled by someone else than by oneself. Better to be oppressed, exploited, persecuted and manipulated by someone other than by oneself.

In this sense the entire movement for liberation and emancipation, inasmuch as it is predicated on a demand for greater autonomy – or, in other words, on a more complete introjection of all forms of control and constraint under the banner of freedom – is a regression. Whatever it may be that comes to us from elsewhere, even the worst exploitation, the very fact that it comes from somewhere else is positive. This is why alienation has its advantages, even though it is so often denounced as the dispossession of the self, with the other treated in consequence as an age-old enemy holding the alienated part of us captive. The inverse theory, that of disalienation, is equally simplistic, holding as it does that the subject merely has to reappropriate his alienated will and his alienated desire. From this perspective everything that befalls the subject as a result of his own efforts is good, because it is authentic; while everything that comes from outside the subject is dubbed inauthentic, merely because it does not fall within the sphere of his freedom.

Exactly the opposite position is the one that has to be stressed, while at the same time broadening the paradox. For just as it is better to be controlled by someone else rather than by oneself, it is likewise always better to be made happy, or unhappy, by someone else rather than by oneself. It is always better to depend in life on something that does not depend on us. In this way I can avoid any kind of servitude. I am not obliged to submit to something that does not depend on me – including my own existence. I am free of my birth – and in the same sense I can be free of my death. There has never been any true freedom apart from this one. The source of all interplay, of everything that is in play, of all passion, of all seduction, is that which is completely foreign to us, yet has power over us. That which is Other, that which we have to seduce.

An ethic founded on the transmission of foreignness implies a philosophy of subtlety. Subtlety as the most basic form of artifice: the subtlety whereby we live not on our own energy or according to our own will but rather thanks to the energy and the will that we *subtly* spirit away from others, from the world, from the whom we love or those whom we hate. We live on a surreptitiously obtained energy, a purloined energy, an energy seduced away from others. The other too, meanwhile, can exist only by means of this subtle and indirect play of capture, seduction and transmission. Placing oneself in the hands of another with respect to will, belief, love or choice is not an abdication but a strategy. In letting your destiny be defined by the other, you draw off the subtlest of energies. By putting some sign or event in charge of your life, you subtly annex the form of that sign or event.

A strategy of this kind is far from innocent. It is the strategy adopted by children. Whereas adults make children believe that they, the adults, are adults, children for their part *let* adults believe that they, the children, are children. Of these two strategies the second is the subtler, for while adults believe that they are adults, children do not believe that they are children. They *are* children, but they do not believe it. They sail under the flag of childhood as under a flag of convenience. The ruse (and the seduction) is total. Children are not far removed, in fact, from Schnitzler's microbes: they are, as it were, a different species, and their vitality and development announce the eventual destruction of the superior – adult – world that surrounds them. Childhood haunts the adult universe as a subtle and deadly presence. It is in this sense that the child is other to the adult: the child is the adult's destiny, the adult is his most subtly distilled form. The child nevertheless repudiates the adult – all the while moving within him with all the grace of those who have no will of their own.

Likewise with the masses, who voyage under this appellation as though in compliance with a destiny of convenience. They too have grown up – in the obscurity of the political realm – as a strange, hostile and unintelligible species whose spontaneous virulence is liable to destroy any political order. They too are the other for authority: a blind protagonist haunting the political labyrinth – that which power cannot know, cannot name, cannot point to. That the masses are able to exert their own subtle power to alter things is due to the fact that they use the same unconscious strategy of letting others want, letting others believe. They themselves are in no danger of believing in their own status as 'masses': since subjectivity and speech are forbidden to them, they have never gone through the political mirror stage. This clearly distinguishes them from the political class, all the members of which believe in – or at least pretend to believe in – the excellence of the said masses. The cynicism of these politicians could never remotely rival the objective cynicism of the masses themselves with regard to their own (non-existent) essence.

The masses thus enjoy a long lead here, for the others *believe* that they, the masses, are alienated – and the masses let them believe it. The feminine principle also partakes of this 'lascivious' irony, as when women let men believe that they are men, while they themselves, secretly, do not believe that they are women (any more than children believe that they are children). One who lets others believe is always superior to one who believes, or makes others believe. The idea of the sexual and political liberation of women was a trap precisely in that it made women believe that they were women. Consequently, the ideology of femininity triumphed: the rights of women, the status of women, the idea of women – all these carried the day, along with the belief in women's own essential nature. Once women are thus 'liberated', once they want to be women, the superior irony of the community of women is perforce lost. No one is immune from this kind of misadventure. Think how men, by taking themselves for free men, have fallen into voluntary servitude.

> The man I am proposing is created externally; he is inauthentic in his very essence, for he is never himself and he is defined by a form which comes into being *between* men. Man is the eternal actor, certainly, but he is also a natural actor, in the sense that his artifice is congenital – this being, indeed, one of his defining human characteristics . . . To be a man means to be an actor, to be a man means to simulate man, to behave like a man, while not being a man deep down: this sums up humanity . . . It is not a matter of urging man to cast aside his mask (behind which there is in any case no face), but what one can ask of man is that he should become aware of his artificial state, and confess it.
>
> If I am condemned to artifice . . .
>
> If it is not given to me to be myself . . .   (Gombrowicz)

Simulating a man, not being oneself, calls for a great deal of affectation. A subtle way of regulating one's fate on the basis of external, 'inauthentic' signs, affectation is condemned by our entire culture, which is a culture of truth and sincerity. Affectation is that affective state in which one becomes aware, as Gombrowicz puts it, of the artificiality of one's condition; in this state we create a kind of artificial double for ourselves, an artificial shadow into which we enter, an artificial automaton produced from our own essence – the means, in short, to externalize ourselves, thanks to signs, as *other*.

Does not great affectation in fact characterize all our automata, all our artificial machines, all our techniques? Andy Warhol has found the formula of maximum snobbery here: 'I want to be a machine'. By assigning himself, as a unique machine, to the realm of machines and machine-made objects, by employing just a touch more simulation and artificiality, Warhol out-manoeuvres the very machinations of this system. Whereas an ordinary machine produces objects, Warhol produces the object's secret aim – which is to be reproduced. He reproduces the object complete with its ultra-purpose, cloaked in the secret non-sense that emanates from the very process of object-generation. Where others seek to add a little soul, Warhol adds a little more machinery. Where others seek a little more meaning, he seeks a little more artifice. Less and less himself, more and more affected, he reaches the machine's magical core by reproducing the world in all its trite exactness. Less and less the subject of desire – closer and closer to the nothingness of the object.

THE OBJECT AS STRANGE ATTRACTOR

In the end, all figures of otherness boil down to just one: that of the Object. In the end, all that is left is the inexorability of the Object, the irredeemability of the Object.

Even at the outer frontiers of science the Object appears ever more ungraspable: it remains internally indivisible and hence unanalysable, infinitely versatile, reversible, ironic, and contemptuous of all attempts to manipulate it. The subject tries desperately to follow it, even at the cost of abandoning scientific principles, but the Object transcends even the sacrifice of scientific rationality. The Object is an insoluble enigma, because it is not itself and does not know itself. It resembles Chesterton's savage, whom one could not understand for the same reason that he could not understand himself. It thus constitutes an obstacle to all understanding. The Object's power and sovereignty derive from the fact that it is estranged from itself, whereas for us the exact opposite is true. Civilization's first gesture is to hold up a mirror to the Object, but the Object is only seemingly reflected therein; in fact it is the Object itself which is the mirror, and it is here that the subject is taken in by the illusion of himself.

So where is science's 'other'? Where is its object? Science has lost its interlocutor, which, like the 'savage', appears not to have responded with genuine dialogue. It seems that it is not a good object, that it does not respect 'difference', that it secretly evades all attempts at scientific evangelization (rational objectification), and that it is taking its revenge for having been 'understood' by surreptitiously undermining the foundations of the edifice of science. The diabolical pursuit-race of the Object and the subject of science is an event worth following.

All that remains is the Object as a strange attractor. The subject is no longer a strange attractor. We know the subject too well; the subject knows himself too well. It is the Object that is exciting, because the Object is my vanishing point. The Object is what theory can be for reality: not a reflection but a challenge, and a strange attractor. This, potentially, is the way to go in search of otherness.

There are two methods of getting beyond alienation. Either disalienation and the reappropriation of oneself – a tiresome process, without much prospect of success these days. Or the other extreme – the path of the absolute Other, of absolute exoticism. This alternative path leads to an exponential defined elsewhere, virtually, in terms of total excentricity. It goes beyond alienation but in the same direction – to what is more other than the Other, to radical otherness.

The duality of otherness implies an unchallengeable metamorphosis, an unchallengeable supremacy of appearances and metamorphoses. I am not alienated. Rather, I am definitively other. No longer subject to the law of desire, but subject now to the total artifice of rules. I have lost any trace of desire of my own. I answer only to something non-human – something inscribed not within me but solely in the objective and arbitrary vicissitudes of the world's signs.

Just as what we deem fatal in catastrophes is the world's sovereign indifference to us, so what we deem fatal in seduction is the Other's sovereign otherness with respect to us. That otherness which erupts into our life, with stunning clarity, in the shape of a gesture, a face, a form, a word, a prophetic dream, a witticism, an object, a woman, or a desert.

This other, when it makes its appearance, is immediately in possession of everything that it will never be given to us to know. This other is the locus of our secret, of everything in us that no longer belongs to the realm of the true. This other is thus not, as in love, the locus of our alikeness, nor, as in alienation, the locus of our difference; neither the ideal image of what we are nor the obscure model of what we lack. Rather, this other is the locus of what escapes us, and the way whereby we escape from ourselves. The other here is not the locus of desire, not the locus of alienation, but the locus of vertiginousness, of eclipse, of appearing and disappearing – the locus, one might say (but we must not), of the scintillation of being. For the rule of seduction is, precisely, secrecy, and the secret in question is that of the fundamental rule.

Seduction knows that the other is never the end of desire, that the subject is mistaken when he focuses on what he loves, just as an utterance is mistaken when it focuses on what it says. Secrecy here is always the secrecy of artifice. The necessity of always focusing somewhere else, of never seeking the other in the terrifying illusion of dialogue but instead following the other like the other's own shadow, and circumscribing him. Never being oneself – but never being alienated either: coming from without to inscribe oneself upon the figure of the Other, within that strange form from elsewhere, that secret form which orders not only chains of events but also existences in their singularity.

The Other is what allows me not to repeat myself for ever.